A KEYWORD DICTIONARY

Edited by
Alasdair Anderson
with Iseabail Macleod

Illustrated by
Barry Rowe

Schofield & Sims Ltd. Huddersfield England

© Schofield & Sims Ltd., 1994

All rights reserved.
No part of this publication may be reproduced, stored in a retrieval system, or transmitted, in any form or by any means, electronic, mechanical, photocopying, recording or otherwise, without the prior permission of Schofield & Sims Ltd.

0 7217 0677 0

First printed 1994
Reprinted 1997

Keyword Dictionary Exercises   0 7217 0678 9

A book of exercises based on this dictionary is also available.

Design and Reprographics by Armitage Typo/Graphics Ltd., Huddersfield
Printed and Bound in Italy by STIGE, Turin

A a

abbey
a place where monks or nuns live.
ability
being able to do things.
abolish
to get rid of something.
above
1 over.
2 higher than.
abroad
in or to another country.
absent
not here, not present.
absolutely
completely, quite.
accent
the way people speak a language.
accept
to take something which is offered or given.
accident
something bad that happens by chance.
accurate
exactly right.
accuse
to say that someone has done something wrong.
ace
a high-scoring playing card.
ache
a pain in some part of the body.
achieve
to manage to do something, usually with effort.
acid
a strong liquid that can burn things.

abbey

absent

ace

a b c d e f g h i j k l m n o p q r s t u v w x y z

acorn

acorn
the seed of the oak tree.

acrobat
someone who does leaping and balancing tricks (in a circus, for example).

act
1 to do something.
2 a part of a play.
3 to perform on stage.

active
lively.

actor
a man who performs in a play, a film or on television.

actress
a woman who performs in a play, a film or on television.

add
1 to put together with something else.
2 to find the total of two or more numbers.

adder
a small, poisonous snake found in Great Britain.

address
the house, street and town where you live.

admiral
the most important officer in a navy.

admire
to think well of someone or something.

admit
1 to agree that something has happened or is true.
2 to allow somebody or something to enter.

adopt
to take someone else's child into your family and care for him or her as if he or she were your own.

adore
to love very much.

adult
a grown-up person.

acorns

acrobat

address

A B C D E F G H I J K L M N O P Q R S T U V W X Y Z

adventure

adventure
an exciting happening.

advertise
to make something well-known (on television, for example).

advertisement
a way of making something known to a lot of people.

advice
what you say to someone to help them.

advise
to tell other people what you think they should do.

aerial
a wire which sends out or picks up radio or television signals.

aeroplane
a flying machine with wings.

affect
to cause things or people to change.

affectionate
showing love for somebody.

afford
to be able to pay for.

afraid
frightened, full of fear.

afternoon
the time of the day between morning and evening.

again
once more.

against
1 on the opposite side, for example in a fight or a game.
2 next to and touching someone or something.

age
1 how old a person is.
2 a special time in history such as the **Stone Age**.

ago
in the past.

advertisement

aerials

afraid

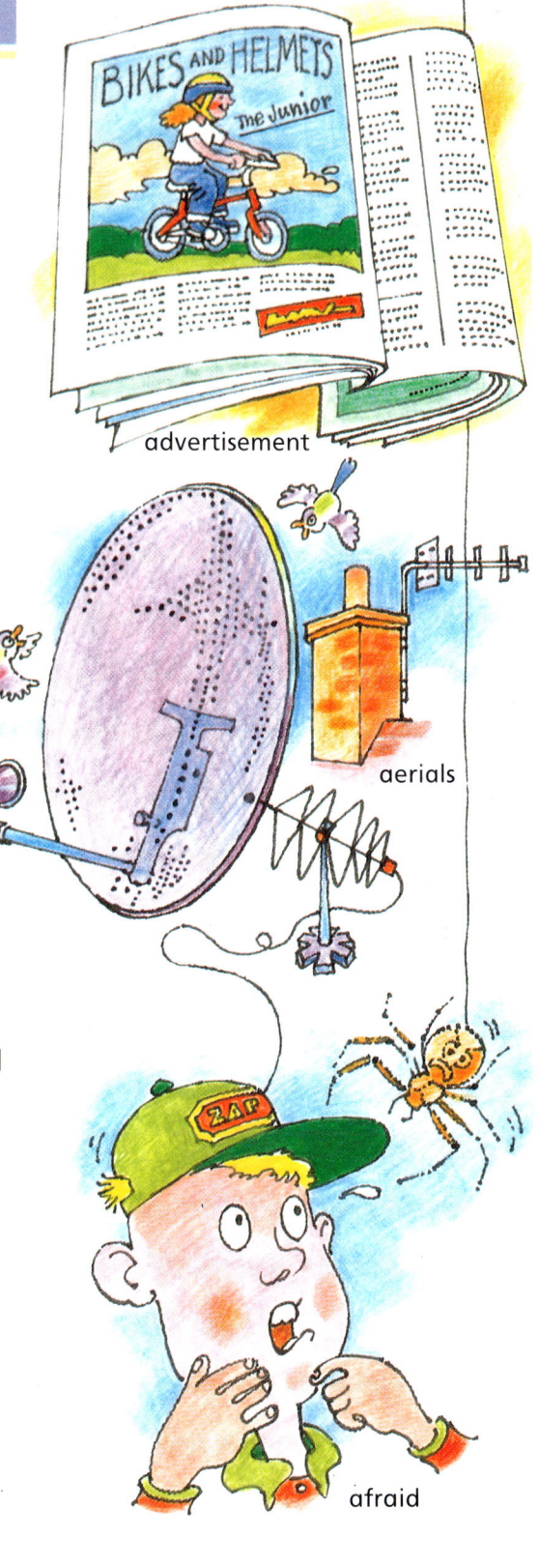

a b c d e f g h i j k l m n o p q r s t u v w x y z

agony

agony
  very great pain.
agree
  to think the same as.
aid
  help.
aim
  1 to try to do something.
  2 **aim at** to point at, for example with a gun.
air
  1 what you breathe.
  2 to make a room fresh by opening a window, for example.
  3 to dry clothes by warming them or putting them in the air.
aircraft
  a flying machine such as an aeroplane or helicopter.
airport
  a place where aircraft land and take off.
alarm
  1 a warning bell or other sound.
  2 a sudden fright.
album
  1 a book with a collection of things such as stamps in it.
  2 a long-playing record.
alike
  the same, similar.
alive
  living, not dead.
alligator
  a kind of crocodile.
allow
  to let someone do something.
almond
  a kind of nut, often used in cooking.
almost
  nearly, not quite.
alone
  by yourself, without other people.

airport

alike

alone

ABCDEFGHIJKLMNOPQRSTUVWXYZ

along

along
from one end to the other.
aloud
in a voice loud enough to be heard.
alphabet
the letters of a language in a fixed order, A, B, C and so on.
already
1 by this time.
2 before this.
altar
the holy table in a church.
alter
to make something different in some way, to change.
although
even if, though.
altogether
counting everybody or everything.
aluminium
a light, silvery-coloured metal.
always
for ever, at all times.
amazing
very surprising.
ambitious
keen to do well at something.
ambulance
a van specially made to carry sick or injured people.
amen
the ending of a prayer.
ammunition
things you can throw or shoot from a weapon to hurt others.
amount
a quantity, a sum (of money, for example).
amuse
to make someone laugh or smile.
ancestor
someone in your family who lived before you.

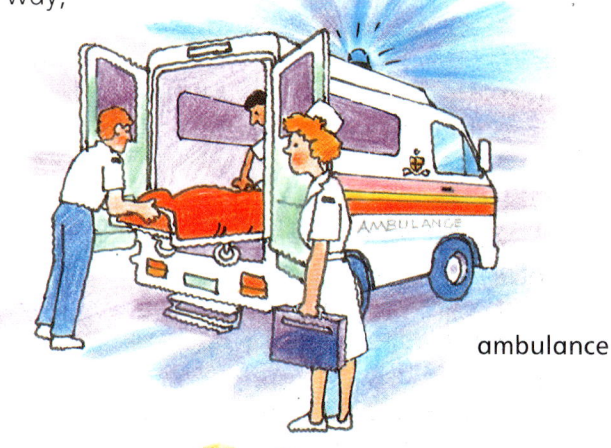

alter

ambulance

ancestor

a b c d e f g h i j k l m n o p q r s t u v w x y z

anchor

anchor
　a heavy metal hook to stop a ship from moving.
ancient
　very old, belonging to long ago.
angel
　someone who is believed to bring messages from God.
angry
　in a bad temper.
animal
　a living creature that can move.
ankle
　the joint between the leg and the foot.
announce
　to say something to a lot of people.
annoy
　to make somebody upset or angry.
annual
　1 happening every year.
　2 a book which comes out each year.
anorak
　a kind of waterproof jacket with a hood.
another
　1 one more.
　2 a different one.
answer
　what you say or write when asked a question.
ant
　a kind of small insect that lives in large groups.
antelope
　an animal like a deer, found in Africa.
anxious
　worried.
ape
　a kind of monkey with no tail or only a very short tail.
apologise
　to say you are sorry for something you have done wrong.

anchors

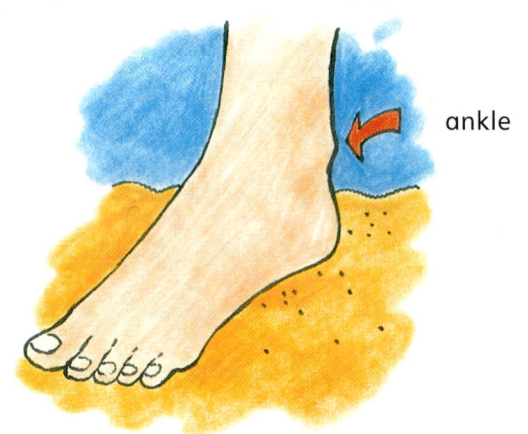

ankle

ants

ABCDEFGHIJKLMNOPQRSTUVWXYZ

appeal

appeal
 to ask for something needed.

appear
 1 to come into view.
 2 to seem to be.

appetite
 the wish to eat.

applaud
 to clap your hands together to show pleasure.

apple
 a kind of round, hard fruit.

appointment
 a time set aside to see someone (for example, a dentist).

approach
 to come near to.

apricot
 a round, soft, yellow fruit with a large, hard seed in it.

apron
 a piece of cloth you wear on top of your clothes to keep them clean.

aquarium
 a glass or plastic container in which fish are kept.

arch
 a curved part of a building or bridge.

architect
 a person who makes the plans for a building.

area
 1 a piece of land or sea.
 2 the size of a surface.

argument
 a disagreement, a fight with words.

arithmetic
 working in numbers, adding, subtracting, multiplying and dividing.

arm
 the part of the body between the shoulder and the hand.

apple

apricot

apron

arithmetic

a b c d e f g h i j k l m n o p q r s t u v w x y z

armour

armour
a covering of metal worn by soldiers in battle.

army
a large number of soldiers.

arrange
1 to put in the right order.
2 to make plans for.

arrest
to make someone a prisoner.

arrive
to reach the place you are going to.

arrow
1 the straight, sharp piece of wood which is shot from a bow.
2 a sign shaped like an arrow to show direction.

art
the making of pictures or sculpture.

article
1 a thing.
2 a piece of writing in a newspaper or magazine.

artificial
not natural, made by people.

artist
a person who makes pictures or sculpture.

ash
1 the grey powder left after a fire.
2 a kind of large tree.

ashamed
to feel bad about something you have done wrong.

ashore
on land.

ask
1 to put a question to.
2 **ask for** to say that you want something.

asleep
sleeping.

assist
to help.

armour

arrow

asleep

A B C D E F G H I J K L M N O P Q R S T U V W X Y Z

astonish

astonish
   to surprise very much.
astronaut
   someone who flies in a spacecraft.
athletics
   sports such as running, jumping or throwing things.
atlas
   a book of maps.
atmosphere
   the air round the earth.
attach
   to fix onto something.
attack
   to start a fight.
attempt
   to try.
attend
   1 to be present.
   2 **attend to** to look after.
attention
   care given to doing a job, listening with care.
attic
   a room just under the roof of a house.
attract
   1 to win the liking of.
   2 to make things come closer.
audience
   people who listen to or watch something (a play or a concert, for example).
aunt
   a father's or mother's sister; the wife of an uncle.
author
   a person who writes books.
autograph
   a person's name written by himself or herself.
automatic
   working by itself.

athletics

attach

attic

a b c d e f g h i j k l m n o p q r s t u v w x y z   11

autumn

autumn
  the season between summer and winter.
avalanche
  a large amount of snow suddenly rushing down a mountainside.
avenue
  a road, often with trees along the sides.
average
  usual, ordinary.
avoid
  to keep away from.
awake
  not sleeping.
award
  a prize for something you have done.
away
  not here; not present.
awful
  very bad.
awkward
  1 clumsy.
  2 difficult to use or deal with.
axe
  a sharp-edged piece of metal on a long handle, used for chopping wood.
axle
  the bar that joins the wheels of a car or cart, for example.

avalanche

avenue

axle

ABCDEFGHIJKLMNOPQRSTUVWXYZ

Bb

baby
a very young child.

back
1 the part opposite to the front.
2 the part of the body between the neck and the bottom of the spine.

backbone
the long row of bones down the middle of your back, the spine.

bacon
salted or smoked meat from the back or sides of a pig.

bad
not good.

badge
a special sign you wear to show your school or club, for example.

badger
an animal with a black and white face which burrows in the ground.

badminton
a game like tennis, played indoors.

bag
a container with a top which can be opened.

bail
1 a small piece of wood placed on the stumps at cricket.
2 **bail out** to empty water from the bottom of a boat.

bait
something used in a trap or on a hook to attract an animal or a fish.

bake
to cook in an oven.

balance
1 to stay steady.
2 a machine for weighing things.

back

bags

balance

a b c d e f g h i j k l m n o p q r s t u v w x y z

balcony

balcony
 1 a raised floor with seats in a theatre or cinema.
 2 a platform outside a window.

bald
 having no hair on the head.

ball
 1 a round object, often used in games.
 2 a special event with dancing.

ballet (say 'ba̲lay')
 a kind of graceful dance which often tells a story.

balloon
 1 a toy of thin rubber which can be blown up.
 2 a round bag which rises when filled with hot air or gas.

bamboo
 a kind of grass with stiff, hollow stems.

ban
 not to allow something.

banana
 a long, curved fruit with a yellow skin.

band
 1 a group of musicians playing together.
 2 a strip of material used to hold things together or as a decoration.
 3 a group of people.

bandage
 a strip of material used to wind round a cut or wound to protect it.

bandit
 a thief, a robber.

bang
 1 a sharp blow.
 2 a sudden, loud noise.

bangle
 a bracelet.

banister
 a handrail beside a staircase.

bank
 1 the side of a river.
 2 a place where money is looked after.
 3 a pile of earth or sand with sloping sides.

balcony

bang

bank

14 A B C D E F G H I J K L M N O P Q R S T U V W X Y Z

banner

banner
a flag hanging from a pole, mast or rope.

banquet
a feast; a large public meal.

bar
1 a rod of metal or wood.
2 a division in music.
3 a counter where drinks and sometimes food are served.

bare
1 having no clothes or covering on, naked.
2 empty.

bargain
something bought cheaply.

barge
a boat with a flat bottom, used on a canal or river.

bark
1 the noise made by a dog.
2 the hard covering round a tree or branch.

barley
a kind of grain used as food and in making beer and whisky.

barn
a building on a farm (used to store grain, for example).

barrel
1 a large, round container, flat at each end.
2 the long tube of a gun out of which the bullets are fired.

barrier
something put up to stop you going somewhere (for example, a fence or a gate).

barrow
a small cart that is pushed.

base
1 the bottom part.
2 where someone or something started out from.

basement
a room or space under a building, a cellar.

banner

barge

barrier

a b c d e f g h i j k l m n o p q r s t u v w x y z

basin

basin
    a wide, round bowl, usually for washing in.

basket
    a bag or container, usually made of woven cane or straw.

basketball
    a game in which two teams each try to throw a ball through a metal hoop.

bat
    1 the piece of wood used to strike a ball (in cricket, for example).
    2 a small, mouse-like animal that flies at night.

bath
    a water container you can lie or sit in to wash yourself.

bathe
    1 to swim or play in water.
    2 to wash (a wound, for example).

battery
    a closed container which stores electricity.

battle
    a fight between two large groups of people.

bay
    a place where the shore curves inwards.

bazaar
    1 a sale of goods to raise money (for a church or school, for example).
    2 a market in Eastern countries.

beach
    land by the sea or by a lake, covered with sand or small stones.

bead
    a small piece of coloured glass, wood or plastic, for example, which can be threaded onto a string.

beak
    the hard, pointed mouth of a bird.

beam
    1 a large, heavy piece of wood or metal used to support something.
    2 a ray of light.

basket

bats

beaks

bean

bean
a seed of the bean plant, used for food.

bear
1 a kind of large, hairy animal with very strong teeth and claws.
2 to carry.
3 to put up with.

beard
hair growing on a man's face.

beast
an animal.

beat
1 to hit again and again.
2 to keep time in music with a stick.
3 to do better than someone in a game or fight.

beautiful
very pretty, very pleasing to see or hear.

beaver
a kind of furry animal with a wide, flat tail which lives in or near water in cool lands.

bed
1 a piece of furniture for sleeping on.
2 a part of a garden where plants are grown.
3 the bottom of the sea or of a river.

bee
an insect which makes honey and has a sting.

beech
a kind of tree with smooth, grey bark.

beef
meat from cattle.

beer
a strong drink made from barley.

beetle
an insect with wings which fold to form a hard back when it is not flying.

beetroot
a dark-red vegetable used in salads.

beg
to ask someone for money or goods.

beggar

beggar
someone who lives by begging.

begin
to start.

behave
to act in a certain way, especially to act well towards others.

behaviour
the way you behave.

behind
at the back of.

being
something that is alive.

believe
to feel sure that something is true, to trust in something.

bell
1 a piece of rounded metal which rings when you hit it.
2 something electrical which is rung to attract attention (for example, a **doorbell**).

belong
1 to be your own.
2 to be a part of.

below
lower down.

belt
a narrow strip of material, worn round the waist.

bench
1 a long, wooden seat.
2 a work-table.

bend
1 a turn, a curve (in a road, for example).
2 to make something turned or curved.

benefit
to do good to.

berry
a small, juicy fruit.

beside
at the side of, next to.

doorbell

belt

bend

A B C D E F G H I J K L M N O P Q R S T U V W X Y Z

better

better
1 finer than, nicer than.
2 less ill than you were.

between
1 in the middle of two things or people.
2 shared by two people.

beware
to be very careful of.

Bible
the religious book of the Christians.

bicycle
a two-wheeled machine you sit on to ride.

bill
1 a piece of paper that shows the money you owe for something.
2 a bird's beak.

bin
a large container for putting rubbish in.

bind
to wrap round with rope or string, for example.

binoculars
a special pair of glasses to let you see far into the distance.

birch
a kind of tree with a silvery-coloured bark.

bird
a feathered animal which has wings and can usually fly.

birthday
the day of the year when a person was born.

biscuit
a thin, dry cake.

bishop
1 the priest in charge of a large district such as a city.
2 a chess piece.

bit
1 a small piece.
2 a piece of metal which is part of a horse's bridle and is held in the mouth.

beware

bin

binoculars

a b c d e f g h i j k l m n o p q r s t u v w x y z   19

bite

bite
  to cut into something with the teeth.
bitter
  tasting sour, not sweet.
black
  the darkest colour, the opposite of white.
blackberry
  a kind of wild, juicy fruit used as food.
blackbird
  a kind of songbird. The male has black feathers.
blackboard
  a board used for writing on with chalk.
blacksmith
  someone who makes things out of iron (for example, horseshoes).
blade
  the sharp part of a knife or sword used for cutting.
blame
  to find fault with, to say who has done wrong.
blank
  empty, with nothing written on it.
blanket
  a warm bed-covering, usually made of wool.
blast
  1 a sudden rush of wind.
  2 to break something up by explosions.
blaze
  to burn with bright flames.
blazer
  a kind of jacket, often with a badge on its top pocket.
bleat
  the sound made by sheep and lambs.
bleed
  to lose blood.
blend
  to mix together.

blacksmith

blank

blaze

blind

blind
    1 not able to see.
    2 a covering for a window.

blindfold
    a covering for the eyes to stop someone seeing.

blink
    to open and close the eyes quickly.

blister
    a sore swelling on the skin with liquid inside it.

blizzard
    a heavy snowstorm with a strong wind.

block
    1 a thick piece of something (for example, wood or stone).
    2 to be in the way of.
    3 a large building with a lot of flats or offices.

blond, blonde
    fair in colour.

blood
    the red liquid which moves round your body.

blossom
    the flowers of plants and trees.

blot
    a dirty mark, especially an ink stain.

blouse
    a light piece of clothing worn by women and girls on the top part of the body.

blow
    1 to shoot air out of the mouth.
    2 (of air) to move quickly.
    3 a hit made with the hand or a weapon.

blue
    the colour of the sky without clouds.

bluebell
    a kind of wild spring flower with small, blue, bell-shaped flowers.

blunder
    a stupid mistake.

blindfold

blow

bluebell

blunt

blunt
not able to cut, not sharp.

blush
when your face goes red because you are embarrassed or shy.

board
1 a flat piece of wood.
2 to go on to (a ship, a train or an aeroplane, for example).

boast
to speak too proudly about yourself or something that belongs to you.

boat
a small ship.

body
1 the whole of a person or animal which can be seen.
2 the body without the head, arms and legs.

bodyguard
a person or group whose job it is to keep someone safe from attack.

bog
wet earth, a swamp.

boil
1 to heat water until it turns to steam.
2 to cook in hot water.
3 a painful swelling under the skin.

bold
brave, not afraid.

bolt
1 a fastener on a door.
2 a metal screw.
3 to rush away.

bomb
a shell which explodes.

bone
one of the hard parts of the body which make up the skeleton.

bonfire
a large fire built in the open air.

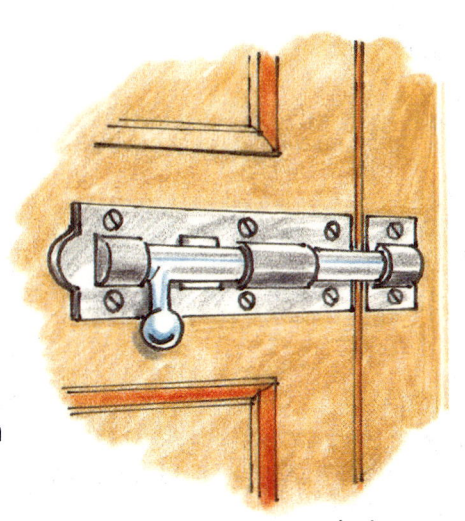

board

boil

bolt

bonnet

bonnet
   1 the cover of a motor car engine.
   2 a kind of hat.

book
   1 a number of pages fastened together.
   2 to arrange for a seat to be kept for you (at the cinema, for example).

boom
   a loud, hollow noise.

boot
   1 a foot covering which comes above the ankles.
   2 a covered place for luggage in a car.

border
   1 the edge of something.
   2 the line where two countries meet.

bore
   1 to make a hole.
   2 to make someone fed up by talking in a dull way.

born
   when something or somebody comes into life.

borrow
   to use something belonging to someone else with their agreement.

bother
   1 trouble.
   2 to annoy.

bottle
   a container for liquids, usually with a narrow neck.

bottom
   1 the lowest part of something.
   2 the part of your body you sit on.

boulder
   a large stone or rock.

bounce
   to make something spring up and down.

bound
   1 to spring upwards and forwards.
   2 tied together.
   3 **bound to** very likely to.

bonnet

boot

boulder

boundary

boundary
 1 the outside edge (of a cricket field, for example).
 2 the line where one piece of land touches another.

bouquet
 a special bunch of flowers.

bow (rhymes with 'low')
 1 ribbon with loops on it.
 2 a weapon used to fire arrows.
 3 the stick used when playing a violin.

bow (rhymes with 'now')
 1 the front part of a boat.
 2 to bend forward from the waist to show respect.

bowl
 1 a deep, round dish.
 2 to send the ball to the person batting (at cricket, for example).
 3 the ball used in the game of bowls.

bowls
 a game in which a large heavy ball is rolled along the grass.

box
 1 a container, usually with a lid, often made of wood, cardboard or metal.
 2 to fight with the fists.

boy
 a young, male child.

bracelet
 a decoration worn on the wrist or arm.

brag
 to boast a lot.

brain
 the part of the head used for thinking.

brake
 the part on a vehicle which makes it go slower or stop.

bramble
 a prickly bush on which blackberries grow.

branch
 the part of the tree on which the leaves grow.

bouquet

box

branch

ABCDEFGHIJKLMNOPQRSTUVWXYZ

brand

brand
    the name of a particular kind of goods made by one company.

brass
    a yellowish metal made by mixing copper and zinc.

brave
    not afraid, ready to face up to danger or pain.

bread
    a baked food made from flour, yeast and water.

break
    1 to cause something to fall to pieces.
    2 a short rest from what you are doing.

breakfast
    the first meal of the day.

breast
    the front, upper part of the body.

breath
    air taken in and let out of your mouth and lungs.

breathe
    to take air in and let it out of your lungs.

breed
    1 the family or kind of an animal.
    2 to have and bring up young ones.

breeze
    a gentle wind.

bribe
    to give someone money so that they will help you dishonestly.

brick
    1 a baked clay block used for building.
    2 a plastic or wooden block used as a toy.

bride
    a woman on her wedding day.

bridegroom
    a man on his wedding day.

bridesmaid
    a girl or young woman who attends a bride at her wedding.

brave

break

bricks

bridge

bridge
   1 something built to let you cross over a river, a road, or a railway.
   2 where the captain stands on a ship.

bridle
   leather straps put on a horse's head to control it.

brief
   short.

briefs
   short underpants.

bright
   1 shining.
   2 clever.

brilliant
   1 very bright, shining.
   2 very clever.

brim
   1 the top edge of a container such as a basin.
   2 the part of a hat which sticks out at the edge.

bring
   to take with you.

brisk
   quick, lively.

bristles
   short, stiff hairs like those on a brush.

broad
   very wide.

broken
   in pieces.

bronze
   a metal made by mixing copper and tin.

brooch (say 'broach')
   an ornament which can be pinned to your clothing.

brood
   1 a number of young birds hatched together.
   2 to think deeply and to worry, often when there is no need to do so.

bridges

broad

brooch

A B C D E F G H I J K L M N O P Q R S T U V W X Y Z

broom

broom
   a stiff brush with a long handle.

brother
   a boy or man who has the same parents as someone else.

brow
   1 the forehead.
   2 the top of a hill.

brown
   the colour of earth or of chocolate.

bruise
   a mark on the skin where it has been hit.

brush
   1 a tool used for sweeping, scrubbing and painting.
   2 a fox's tail.

bubble
   1 a hollow ball of liquid filled with air or gas.
   2 to give off bubbles, like water when it boils.

bucket
   a container with a handle, often used for carrying liquids, a pail.

buckle
   a fastener for a belt or shoe, for example.

bud
   a leaf or flower before it opens.

budgerigar
   a kind of small, brightly-coloured bird often kept as a pet.

bugle
   a musical wind instrument like a small trumpet.

build
   to put up; to make into something.

building
   something built with walls and a roof.

bulb
   1 a rounded plant root (for example, an onion).
   2 the part of an electric light that shines.

brushes

bubbles

build

a b c d e f g h i j k l m n o p q r s t u v w x y z

bulge

bulge
to swell outwards.
bull
a male animal of cattle and some other animals.
bulldozer
a large machine for moving earth.
bullet
a piece of metal shot from a gun.
bully
someone who hurts or frightens weaker people.
bump
1 a sudden knock.
2 a swelling on the body where it has been hit.
bumper
a metal or plastic rail at the front and back of a vehicle.
bun
a kind of small, round cake.
bunch
several things tied together.
bundle
many things tied or held together.
bungalow
a house by itself with all its rooms on one floor.
bunk
a bed sometimes fixed to a wall like a shelf, often with another above.
buoy (say 'boy')
a fixed floating object which is placed somewhere to warn ships of danger.
burglar
a person who enters houses and shops to steal.
burial
the burying of a dead body.
burn
1 to be or to set on fire.
2 a sore place on the skin caused by heat.

bull

bungalow

buoy

burrow

burrow
    an underground tunnel dug by an animal such as a rabbit.

burst
    1 to blow into pieces.
    2 to break open.

bury
    to put something in a hole in the ground and cover it over.

bus
    a large motor vehicle which carries passengers.

bush
    a small tree.

business
    work, trade.

busy
    having no time to spare, doing a lot of things.

butcher
    a person who sells meat.

butter
    a fatty food made from cream.

buttercup
    a kind of bright-yellow wild flower.

butterfly
    a kind of insect with four large wings, often brightly coloured.

button
    a fastening which fits into a hole, used on clothing.

buy
    to get something by giving money.

buzz
    a low sound such as that made by some insects when flying.

bus

busy

butterfly

a b c d e f g h i j k l m n o p q r s t u v w x y z   29

Cc

cab
1 a place for the driver of a lorry or train.
2 a taxi.

cabbage
a kind of large, usually green, broad-leaved vegetable.

cabin
1 a room on a boat or an aeroplane.
2 a small, wooden house.

cable
1 wires that carry electricity or telephone calls.
2 a strong rope often made of wires twisted together.

cackle
to laugh making a noise like a hen after it lays an egg.

cactus
a prickly desert plant with thick stems.

café
a place for eating simple meals or snacks.

cage
a box or room made of wires or bars in which animals or birds are kept.

cake
a sweet, baked food made of flour, eggs and sugar, for example.

calculator
a small machine used to work out very large or complicated sums.

calendar
a sheet or book showing the days, weeks and months of the year.

calf
1 a young animal, usually a young cow or bull.
2 the soft back part of the leg between the knee and ankle.

cable

cactus

cage

30 ABCDEFGHIJKLMNOPQRSTUVWXYZ

call

call
   1 to shout to.
   2 to visit.
   3 to give a name to.

calm
   quiet and still, peaceful.

camel
   a kind of humped animal used for carrying people and goods in the desert.

camera
   a machine for taking photographs.

camp
   1 a group of tents together.
   2 to live in a tent.

can
   a small sealed container made of tin.

canal
   a very large ditch filled with water for boats to use.

canary
   a kind of yellow songbird sometimes kept as a pet.

candle
   a stick of wax with a wick which is burned to give light.

cane
   the hollow stalk of some plants, which can be made into a stick.

cannibal
   someone who eats human flesh.

cannon
   a big, heavy gun which fires shells.

canoe
   a light, narrow boat moved by using a paddle.

canteen
   a place where people eat together (in a factory or school, for example).

cap
   1 a kind of head covering.
   2 a lid or cover.

camera

cannon

canoe

a b c d e f g h i j k l m n o p q r s t u v w x y z

cape

cape
  a cloak to cover a person's shoulders and arms.
capital
  1 the chief city or town.
  2 a large letter such as A, B, Y or Z.
captain
  1 the person who controls an aeroplane or a ship.
  2 an officer in the army.
  3 the leader of a team or group.
capture
  to take prisoner, to catch.
car
  a motor vehicle to carry people.
caramel
  a kind of chewy sweet.
caravan
  a house on wheels.
card
  1 a piece of stiff, thick paper.
  2 a piece of card with a message and often a picture.
  3 one of a set of cards used for playing games.
cardboard
  strong, thick paper.
cardigan
  a short woollen jacket.
care
  1 to be concerned about.
  2 the act of looking after someone or something.
caretaker
  a person who looks after a building such as a school.
cargo
  goods carried on a ship or aeroplane.
carnation
  a kind of sweet-smelling garden flower (usually pink, white or red).
carnival
  a large procession, usually in fancy dress.

caravan

card

cardigan

A B C D E F G H I J K L M N O P Q R S T U V W X Y Z

carol

carol
a Christmas song.

carpenter
someone who makes things out of wood.

carpet
a thick, soft covering for a floor.

carriage
1 a part of a train where people sit.
2 a vehicle pulled by horses.

carrot
a long, orange root vegetable.

carry
to take from one place to another.

cart
a vehicle for carrying goods, often pulled by a horse.

carton
a box made of cardboard.

cartoon
1 a drawing, usually in a comic or newspaper, to make you laugh.
2 a short film made out of drawings.

carve
1 to shape wood or stone with cutting tools.
2 to cut meat into slices.

case
1 a kind of box to keep or carry things in.
2 a suitcase.

cash
money in notes or coins.

cassette
recording tape in a container.

cast
1 people taking part in a play or film.
2 to throw.
3 something shaped in a mould.

castle
an old stone building with strong walls, built to keep out enemies.

catalogue
a list of things in a special order.

carpet

carriage

carry

a b **c** d e f g h i j k l m n o p q r s t u v w x y

catch

catch
1 to take hold of.
2 to get an illness.

caterpillar
a creature, like a worm with legs, which will turn into a moth or butterfly.

cathedral
a very important church.

catkin
a kind of fluffy flower which grows on some trees (for example, the willow).

cauliflower
a vegetable with a hard, white flower which you can eat.

cause
to make something happen.

cautious
taking great care.

cave
a hollow place in rocks or in the earth.

ceiling
the top part of a room.

celebrate
to remember something in a special way, especially by having a party or feast.

celery
a vegetable with long, whitish-green stalks.

cell
a room in which prisoners are kept.

cellar
a room under a building for storing things.

cello
a musical instrument like a large violin.

cement
a stone dust which sets hard when mixed with water.

cemetery
a place where people are buried.

centimetre
a measure of length; 100 of these are equal to a metre.

catkin

celery

cauliflower

cemetery

A B C D E F G H I J K L M N O P Q R S T U V W X Y Z

centipede

centipede
a crawling insect with a large number of legs.

central
1 in the middle.
2 important.

central heating
a way of warming a building by sending heat from a central point through pipes.

centre
1 the middle of something.
2 a place where people come together to do things.

century
a hundred years.

cereal
1 a crop such as wheat, rice or oats used for food.
2 a kind of food made from grain and usually eaten for breakfast.

ceremony
a special event held to celebrate something.

certain
sure.

chaffinch
a kind of small bird.

chain
a number of rings joined together.

chair
a piece of furniture for one person to sit on.

chalk
1 a soft, white rock which crumbles.
2 a white or coloured stick used for writing on a blackboard.

challenge
1 to offer to fight someone.
2 a test of ability.

champion
the winner over all the others in a competition.

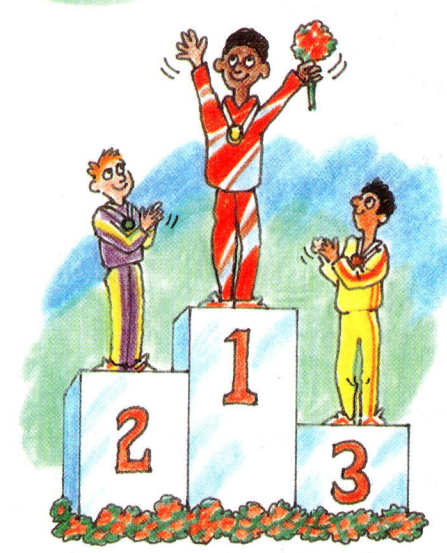

centre

cereal

champion

a b c d e f g h i j k l m n o p q r s t u v w x y z   35

chance

chance
   1 an unexpected happening.
   2 a time when you can do something you want to do.

change
   1 to become different.
   2 money you get back when you pay more than is needed.

chapter
   a part of a story or book.

character
   1 what someone is like as a person.
   2 a person in a play or story.

charge
   1 to rush at.
   2 the price asked for something.
   3 **in charge** in control of something.

charm
   1 a magic spell.
   2 a small ornament which is supposed to bring good luck.

charming
   pleasing to other people.

chase
   to run after.

chat
   to talk in a friendly way.

chatter
   to speak quickly, especially about things that do not matter.

cheap
   low in price, not costing a lot.

cheat
   to act unfairly, to make others believe what is not true.

check
   1 to make sure that everything is in order.
   2 a pattern of squares.

cheek
   1 one of the sides of the face between the nose and the ears.
   2 rudeness.

charge

check

cheek

ABCDEFGHIJKLMNOPQRSTUVWXYZ

cheer

cheer
to shout loudly for joy.

cheerful
full of fun, looking happy.

cheese
a solid food made from milk.

chemist
someone who sells medicines.

cherry
a small, red fruit with a large, hard seed in it.

chess
a game played by two people on a squared board.

chest
1 a large, strong box.
2 the upper front part of the body.

chestnut
the hard, brown seed of the chestnut tree.

chew
to keep biting food in your mouth to crush it.

chick
a young bird.

chicken
a young hen kept for its eggs and meat.

chief
1 the person in charge.
2 the most important.

child
a young boy or girl.

chill
1 coldness.
2 a slight cold which causes shivering.

chilly
(of weather) quite cold.

chime
the noise made by bells.

chimney
a pipe to take smoke away from a fire.

chimpanzee
a kind of intelligent ape.

cheer

chest

chimpanzee

chin

chin
   the part of the face below the bottom lip.

china
   fine pottery, especially cups and saucers and plates.

chip
   1 a tiny piece broken from something larger.
   2 a thin slice of potato fried in deep fat.

chirp
   a noise made by young birds and some insects.

chisel
   a sharp steel tool used for cutting wood, stone or metal.

chocolate
   a sweet food made from cocoa powder.

choice
   the act of choosing; something you choose.

choir
   a group of people singing together.

choke
   1 to be unable to breathe because of something in the throat.
   2 to block up.

choose
   to pick out what is wanted from a large number.

chop
   1 to cut with an axe or knife.
   2 a slice of meat with a bone in it.

chorus
   1 part of a song or poem which is repeated after each verse.
   2 a group of people singing together.

christening
   when a baby is given its name in a Christian church.

Christian
   a believer in Jesus Christ.

chuckle
   to laugh quietly.

china

chisel

choose

chum

chum
   a close friend.

chunk
   a thick piece cut off from something larger.

church
   a building where people, especially Christians, go to worship.

cider
   a strong drink made from apples.

cigar
   dried tobacco leaves rolled tightly together and used for smoking.

cigarette
   cut-up tobacco leaves rolled in a paper tube for smoking.

cinder
   a piece of coal which has been partly burned.

cinema
   a place where films are shown.

circle
   something round.

circus
   a travelling show of acrobats, clowns and sometimes animals.

city
   a very large town.

claim
   to say that something belongs to you.

clang
   the sound made by a large bell.

clap
   1 to slap the hands together quickly.
   2 the sound made by thunder.

clash
   to bump together noisily.

class
   people who are taught together.

clatter
   a loud rattling noise.

church

cinema

clap

claw

claw
    the sharp, hard nails of a bird or an animal.

clay
    sticky earth from which bricks and pottery may be made.

clean
    not dirty or dusty.

clear
    1 easy to see, hear or understand.
    2 to put away, to tidy.

clerk (say 'clark')
    a person who deals with letters, for example, in an office.

clever
    1 quick at learning and understanding things.
    2 skilful.

click
    a small, sharp noise.

cliff
    high, steep land often overlooking the sea.

climate
    the sort of weather a place usually has.

climb
    to go up a steep place.

cling
    to hold on tightly.

clinic
    a place where doctors and nurses give help to people.

clip
    1 a fastener.
    2 to cut with a pair of shears or scissors.

cloak
    a loose covering without sleeves for the body and arms.

clock
    a machine for telling the time.

clockwork
    machinery which is worked by winding a spring.

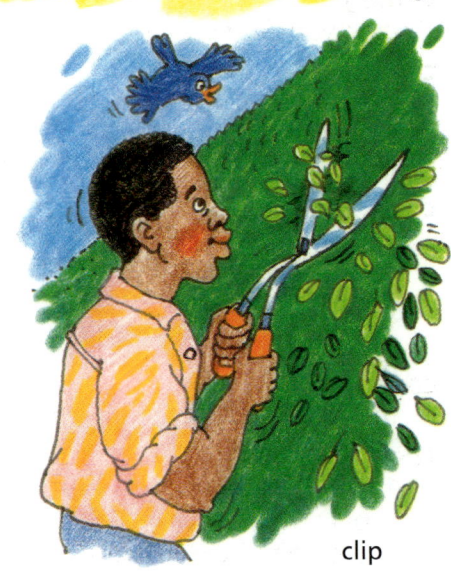

cliff

cling

clip

close

close (rhymes with 'dose')
near.

close (rhymes with 'doze')
to shut.

cloth
1 material for making clothes or curtains, for example.
2 a piece of cloth for cleaning something.

cloud
a mass of rainy mist floating in the sky.

clover
a kind of small flowering plant with leaves in three parts.

clown
a person who acts foolishly to make people laugh.

club
1 a heavy stick.
2 a group of people who meet together for a special purpose.
3 a stick used to play golf.
4 one of the four kinds in a pack of playing cards.

clue
something which helps you to find the answer to a puzzle or a question.

clumsy
awkward in the way you move or do things.

coach
1 a passenger vehicle such as a bus.
2 a person who gives special training (to a football team, for example).

coal
black rock dug out of the ground and burned to make heat.

coarse
rough, not fine.

coast
the strip of land next to the sea.

coat
1 a piece of clothing with sleeves, worn over other clothes.
2 the hair of an animal.

close

clouds

coat

a b **c** d e f g h i j k l m n o p q r s t u v w x y z 41

cobweb

cobweb
    a net made by a spider to trap insects.

cock
    a male bird.

cocoa
    1 a powder made from the seeds of a kind of tree.
    2 a hot drink made from cocoa and milk or water.

coconut
    the very hard, hairy fruit of a kind of palm tree.

cod
    a kind of large sea fish used as food.

code
    writing with a hidden meaning.

coffee
    a drink made from the roasted and crushed seeds of the coffee tree.

coffin
    a box in which a dead body is put.

coil
    to gather rope, wire or piping in rings (one on top of the other).

coin
    a piece of metal used as money.

coke
    1 baked coal from which gas has been taken.
    2 **Coke** a kind of sweet, fizzy drink.

cold
    1 not hot.
    2 an illness which makes your nose run.

collar
    1 a leather or metal band put round the neck of an animal.
    2 the part of your clothes which fits round the neck.

collect
    to gather together.

collection
    a number of things gathered in a set.

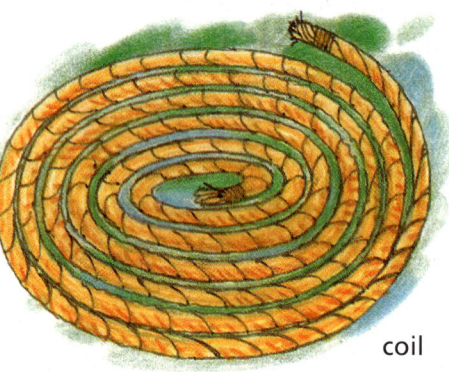

cobweb

coil

collar

ABCDEFGHIJKLMNOPQRSTUVWXYZ

college

college
   a place where students are taught.

collide
   to come together with great force.

colour
   what makes things look green or red, for example.

comb
   a thin piece of metal or plastic with many teeth, used to keep hair tidy.

comedian
   a person who tells funny stories in public to make people laugh.

comedy
   a play or film that makes you laugh.

comfort
   1 a pleasant, easy feeling.
   2 to show kindness to someone in pain or trouble.

comfortable
   giving or having comfort.

comic
   1 making you laugh, funny.
   2 a magazine or paper for young people with stories told in pictures.

command
   order.

commercial
   1 to do with buying and selling.
   2 an advertisement on television, for example.

common
   ordinary, usual; found in many places.

companion
   someone who is with you, often a friend.

company
   1 people you are with.
   2 a group of people doing business, a firm.

compare
   to see if things are alike.

collide

colours

comb

a b **c** d e f g h i j k l m n o p q r s t u v w x y z

compartment

compartment
a separate section (of a refrigerator or a railway carriage, for example).

compass
an instrument which tells you where north is.

competition
a way of finding out who is the best or luckiest at something.

complain
to find fault, to grumble.

complete
1 the whole with nothing missing.
2 to finish altogether.

complicated
having a lot of parts; difficult to understand, not simple.

compliment
something nice someone says to praise you.

composer
a person who makes up music.

computer
a machine that stores information and can work things out quickly.

concentrate
to think hard about something.

concert
music played in front of an audience.

conduct
to guide, to lead.

conductor
a person who is in charge of an orchestra or choir.

confess
to tell about things you have done wrong.

confident
feeling sure or safe.

congratulate
to say you are pleased about something good that has happened to someone.

conjuror
a magician, someone who can do tricks.

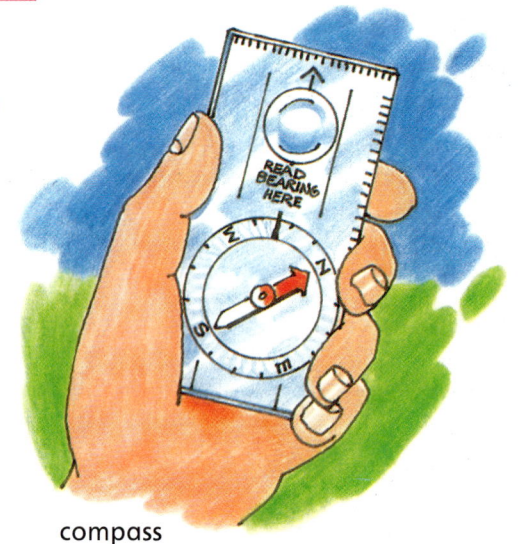

compass

complete

complicated

44 A B **C** D E F G H I J K L M N O P Q R S T U V W X Y Z

connect

connect
 to join together.

conscience
 the feeling inside you which tells you if something is right or wrong.

conscious
 awake, knowing what is happening.

constable
 an ordinary policeman or policewoman.

construct
 to build.

contain
 to have inside, to hold.

container
 something in which other things may be stored (a box, jar, chest or bag, for example).

content (say 'con<u>tent</u>')
 quite pleased, satisfied with things as they are.

contents (say '<u>con</u>tents')
 what something contains.

contest
 a competition to find the best or the winner.

continent
 one of the large land masses of the world, such as Europe, Asia or Africa.

continue
 to go on with, to go on, to last.

control
 to guide; to keep steady.

convenient
 suitable.

conversation
 talk between two or more people.

convince
 to make someone believe something.

cook
 1 to make food ready to eat by heating it (for example, by boiling or frying).
 2 a person who cooks.

connect

constables

conversation

a b **c** d e f g h i j k l m n o p q r s t u v w x y z   45

cool

cool
not quite cold.

copper
1 a reddish-brown metal.
2 the colour of this metal.

copy
1 to do the same as somebody else, to imitate.
2 to make something the same as something else.

cord
a piece of thick string or thin rope.

core
the part in the centre of something (for example, the core of an apple where the seeds are).

cork
1 the light, thick bark of the cork tree.
2 a piece of this or another substance used to close the mouth of a bottle.

corn
1 the seeds of grain used as food.
2 a hard, sore place on the foot.

corner
where two roads, lines or walls meet.

corpse
a dead body.

correct
1 quite right, true.
2 to make something right.

corridor
a narrow, covered passage with doors leading into rooms.

cost
how much you must pay to buy something.

costume
clothes worn for a special reason or occasion (for example, on the stage).

cosy
1 comfortable and warm.
2 a cover for a teapot or a boiled egg.

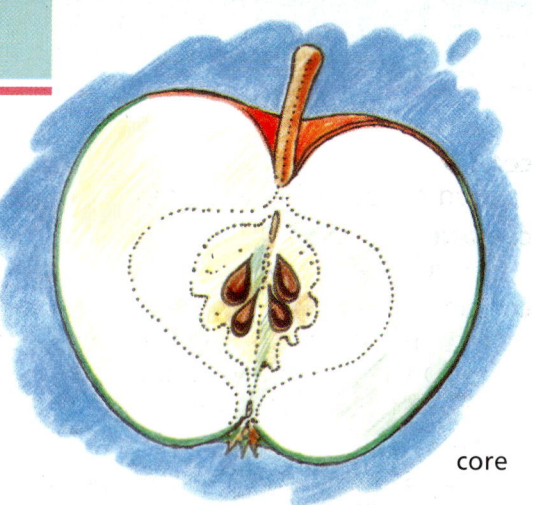

core

corner

corridor

46 A B **C** D E F G H I J K L M N O P Q R S T U V W X Y Z

cot

cot
> a baby's bed with high sides.

cottage
> a small country house.

cotton
> 1 a kind of light cloth made from a plant grown in warm countries.
> 2 thread used for sewing.

couch
> a soft seat for more than one person, a sofa, a settee.

cough
> to force air from the chest and lungs with a noise.

council
> a group of people chosen to plan and decide what should be done in a place.

count
> to number in the proper order, to add up.

counter
> 1 a table over which things are served in a shop.
> 2 a small disc used in counting and in playing games.

country
> 1 the whole of a land, such as Germany or France.
> 2 the part of a land which is away from towns.

county
> a division of England, Wales or Ireland.

couple
> two of anything.

coupon
> a ticket which can be changed for something of value.

courage
> great bravery.

course
> 1 a large stretch of land where certain sports take place, such as a **golf course**.
> 2 a part of a meal.
> 3 the direction something takes.

cottage

counter

golf course

a b c d e f g h i j k l m n o p q r s t u v w x y z   47

court

court
1 a piece of land on which certain games are played (for example, a **tennis court**).
2 a place where trials are held.
3 the place where a king and queen live with the people who help them.

cousin
the child of an uncle or aunt.

cover
to put something over something else.

cow
a large female animal kept on farms for its milk and meat.

coward
a person who runs away from danger or difficulty.

cowboy
a man who rides a horse and looks after cattle in America.

crab
a kind of shellfish with ten legs.

crack
1 to break, to make a slight break in.
2 a sharp noise like something hard breaking.

cradle
a rocking bed for a baby.

craft
a job or trade needing skill, especially with the hands.

crafty
not able to be trusted, cunning.

crane
1 a tall machine for lifting heavy things.
2 a kind of large water bird with long legs.

crash
1 a loud noise made by something breaking.
2 an accident when cars or trains, for example, bang into something.

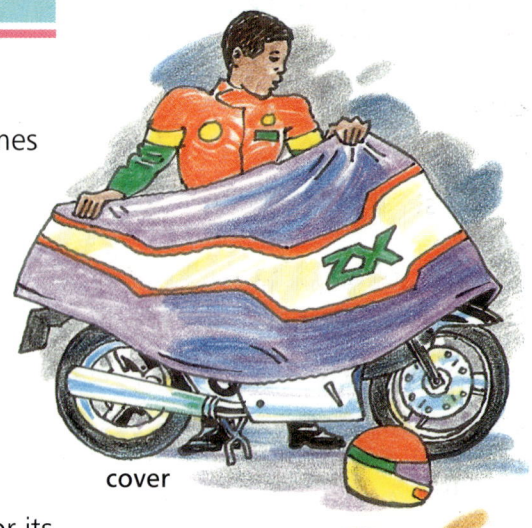

cover

crab

crane

A B **C** D E F G H I J K L M N O P Q R S T U V W X Y Z

crawl

crawl
 1 to move on the hands and knees.
 2 to move slowly.
 3 a stroke used in swimming.

crayon
 a stick of coloured wax for drawing with.

crazy
 1 mad, without sense.
 2 likely to do strange or silly things.

cream
 1 the thick liquid found on the top of milk.
 2 the colour of cream.

crease
 1 the mark made by folding something (cloth, for example).
 2 a special mark on a cricket pitch.

create
 to make something new.

creature
 any living thing.

creep
 1 to move along close to the ground.
 2 to move carefully, often to avoid being seen.

crescent
 1 part of the edge of a circle; the shape of the new moon.
 2 a curved street.

crest
 1 the top of something, especially the top of a wave.
 2 feathers on the top of something.

crew
 a team of people who do the work on a ship or an aircraft, for example.

cricket
 1 a game played with a ball, bat and stumps.
 2 a kind of jumping insect which chirps.

crime
 breaking the law.

criminal
 a person who breaks the law.

crawl

crescent

cricket

a b **c** d e f g h i j k l m n o p q r s t u v w x y z 49

crimson

crimson
    a deep-red colour.

crisp
    1 firm and dry.
    2 a very thin slice of potato cooked in oil.

crocodile
    a large and dangerous animal found in some hot countries, especially in rivers.

crocus
    a kind of small, yellow, purple or white spring flower.

crook
    1 a person who commits a crime, a criminal.
    2 a shepherd's stick with a hook at one end.

crooked
    1 bent, not straight.
    2 dishonest.

crop
    1 plants grown for food.
    2 the amount of such gathered at one time.

cross
    1 anything shaped like ✕ or + .
    2 to move from one side to the other.
    3 angry.

crouch
    to bend down low with your legs bent.

crow
    a kind of large, black bird which has a loud, rough cry.

crowd
    a large number of people all together in one place.

crown
    1 the special head-dress of a king or queen, often made of gold.
    2 the top of an object such as a person's head or a hill.

cruel
    very unkind, without pity.

cruise
    a long journey by boat or aeroplane.

crocodile

crosses

crown

A B C D E F G H I J K L M N O P Q R S T U V W X Y Z

crumb

crumb
 a tiny piece of bread or cake.

crumble
 to break into little pieces

crush
 to press together very tightly, to squash.

crust
 the hard outside part of anything, especially of bread.

crutch
 a wood or metal support used by someone with a hurt leg to help them walk.

cry
 1 to call out.
 2 to have tears in your eyes, to weep.

cub
 a young animal, such as a fox, wolf or lion.

cube
 a solid, square shape.

cuckoo
 a bird which lays its eggs in other birds' nests and makes a sound like its name.

cucumber
 a long, green vegetable often eaten in salads.

cuddle
 to take into the arms and hug closely.

cuff
 the end of a sleeve.

cultivate
 to dig or plough land to grow crops.

cunning
 clever in a sly way.

cupboard
 a set of shelves with doors at the front.

cure
 to make somebody better after an illness.

curious
 1 strange, unusual.
 2 wanting to know.

crutch

cuckoo

cupboard

curls

curls
hair formed into rings.

currant
1 a small, dried grape often used in puddings and cakes.
2 a kind of small berry grown on a bush.

current
a flow of water, air or electricity, for example.

curry
a food with a very hot, spicy taste.

curtain
a cloth which hangs in front of a window, for example.

curve
a smooth, round shape, a smooth bend.

cushion
a pillow which is often used on a chair.

custard
a sweet, yellow sauce which is eaten with puddings.

custom
what is usually done; what usually happens.

customer
a person who buys something in a shop or market.

cut
to open or divide with something sharp.

cutlery
knives, forks and spoons.

cycle
1 a bicycle.
2 to make a bicycle move.

cylinder
a long, round, solid shape, like a soup tin.

cushion

cut

cylinders

Dd

dab
to touch lightly.
Dad, Daddy
a name for your father.
daffodil
a kind of yellow spring flower grown from a bulb.
dagger
a pointed knife with a short blade, sharp on both sides.
daily
each day.
dairy
1 a place where butter and cheese are made from milk and cream.
2 a shop where milk, butter, eggs and cheese are sold.
daisy
a small flower with a yellow centre and white petals.
dam
a wall built to hold back water.
damage
to harm.
damp
slightly wet.
dance
to move on the feet to music.
dandelion
a kind of yellow wild flower.
danger
harm; something that can hurt you.
dangerous
likely to hurt, harm or kill.
dangle
to hang down from something, to swing loosely from something.

daisy

dam

dance

a b c d e f g h i j k l m n o p q r s t u v w x y z   53

dare

dare
1 to be brave enough to do something dangerous.
2 to ask someone to do something dangerous.

dark
without light.

darling
a name for someone you love very much.

dart
1 to move very quickly.
2 a small arrow thrown at a board in a game.

dash
1 to rush from place to place.
2 a short line like this – used in writing.

date
1 the day, month and year when something takes place.
2 a sweet, brown fruit.

daughter
a female child of a parent.

dawn
the very first light of the day, daybreak.

day
1 a period of twenty-four hours.
2 the time between sunrise and sunset.

dazed
not knowing where you are (for example, after a blow on the head).

dazzle
to blind for a moment with bright light.

dead
no longer alive.

deadly
able to cause death.

deaf
not able to hear.

dear
1 much loved by someone.
2 costing a lot of money.

death
when you stop living.

dark

dart

dazzle

debt

debt
what you owe to someone.
decent
proper, respectable.
decide
to make up your mind about something.
deck
the floor of a boat, an aeroplane or a bus.
decorate
1 to paint or paper a room or a house.
2 to make something prettier.
deed
an action, something done.
deep
far down, often in water; far inside.
deer
a large wild animal which can run fast.
defeat
to beat in battle or in a game.
defend
to protect, to guard.
definite
sure, certain.
delay
1 to put off doing something for a while.
2 to make late.
deliberate
done on purpose.
delicate
very fine; easily broken.
delicious
having a very pleasant taste or smell.
delight
great pleasure, joy.
deliver
to bring, to carry.
demand
to ask very firmly for something.
denim
strong cotton cloth which is usually blue.
dense
very thick, too thick to see through.

decorate

deer

delicious

a b c **d** e f g h i j k l m n o p q r s t u v w x y z 55

dentist

dentist
a person who looks after teeth.

deny
to say firmly that something is not true.

depend
to trust somebody or something for help.

depth
how deep something is.

describe
to say how something or someone looks.

description
saying what something is.

desert (say 'desert')
a large, empty place where hardly anything grows because of heat and lack of water.

deserve
to be worthy of, to have earned some reward or punishment.

design
a plan or drawing; a pattern.

desk
a kind of table used for writing at.

desperate
ready to do almost anything to get what you want, because you have lost hope.

dessert (say 'dessert')
the sweet food eaten at the end of a meal.

destroy
to break up completely, to do away with.

detail
a very small part or fact.

detective
a person, usually a policeman, whose job it is to find out who carried out a crime.

detergent
a liquid or powder used for washing (clothes or dishes, for example).

develop
1 to grow, to change gradually.
2 to bring out the picture in a photographic film.

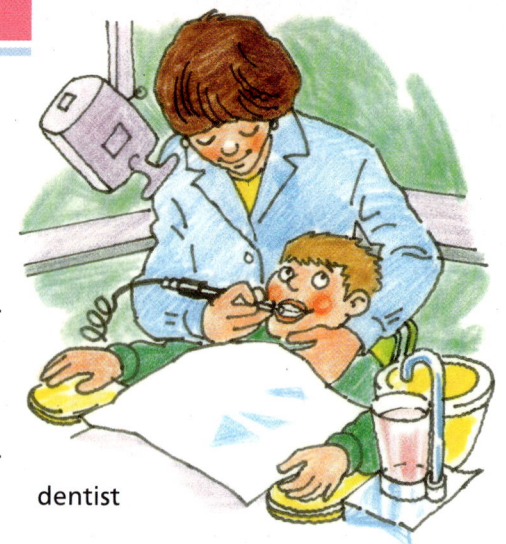

dentist

desk

detergents

dew

dew
    drops of water found on the ground and on plants in the early morning.

dial
    1 the face of an object such as a clock or telephone, with numbers or letters on it.
    2 to enter the number into a telephone.

diamond
    1 a very hard precious stone, often used in rings.
    2 a shape like this ◇, with four sloping sides that are the same length.
    3 a playing card with these shapes.

diary
    a book in which you write what has happened or what is to happen each day.

dice
    a small, square block with numbers on it, used in many games.

dictionary
    a book like this one with a list of words and their meanings, arranged in alphabetical order.

die
    to stop living.

diet
    1 the sort of food we eat.
    2 an eating plan to let you lose weight or be healthier.

different
    not like something else, not the same.

difficult
    not easy to do or to understand.

dig
    to turn soil over.

digest
    to break down food in your stomach after you have eaten it.

dim
    not bright; not easy to see.

din
    a great noise of many things together.

dials

dice

dig

a b c **d** e f g h i j k l m n o p q r s t u v w x y z

dinghy

dinghy
   a small rowing or sailing boat.

dinner
   the main meal of the day.

dip
   1 to place into a liquid for a short time.
   2 to slope downwards.

direct
   1 the shortest and quickest way.
   2 to tell somebody which way to go.

dirt
   mud, dust, something not clean.

dirty
   not clean.

disabled
   not able to use part of your body properly.

disagree
   not to agree with.

disappear
   to go out of sight, to vanish.

disappoint
   to make somebody sorry because they have not got what they hoped for.

disaster
   a terrible event, happening or accident.

disc (also spelt **disk**)
   1 a round, flat object.
   2 a plastic **disk** for storing information in a computer.

disco
   a place where people dance to recorded music.

discover
   to find out about something; to find for the first time.

discuss
   to talk about something with other people.

disease
   an illness.

disgraceful
   very bad, shameful.

dinghy

computer disks

discover

disguise

disguise
 to change your appearance by altering your face and clothes.

disgust
 strong feeling against something.

dish
 1 a bowl or plate.
 2 food served at a meal.

dishonest
 not honest or trustworthy.

disk
 see **disc**.

dislike
 not to like.

display
 a show.

dissolve
 to mix completely with a liquid.

distance
 1 somewhere far away.
 2 the space between two points or places.

district
 a part of a country or a town.

disturb
 1 to upset, to worry.
 2 to put out of order.

ditch
 a long, narrow hole dug in the ground, usually to let water flow away.

dive
 to jump into water head first.

diver
 someone wearing special equipment who works under water.

divide
 1 to share between; to split up.
 2 to work out how many times one number goes into another.

dizzy
 unsteady, feeling as though you are spinning round.

ditch

dive

dizzy

a b c **d** e f g h i j k l m n o p q r s t u v w x y z   59

dock

dock
1 the place where boats are loaded and unloaded.
2 the place where a prisoner stands in a court of law.

doctor
a person who looks after people's health.

dodge
to move quickly from one side to the other; to avoid.

doe
a female deer or rabbit.

dog
a four-legged animal often kept as a pet.

doll
a model of a real person used as a toy.

dollar
a form of money used in some countries, such as America or Canada.

dolphin
a kind of warm-blooded sea animal.

domino
an oblong piece of wood or plastic with dots on it, used in the game of **dominoes**.

donkey
an animal like a small horse with long ears.

door
1 an entrance to a room or a building.
2 the part of a cupboard or wardrobe that opens.

dormitory
a large room containing several beds.

dose
the amount of medicine that you should take at one time.

dot
a tiny round mark or point.

double
twice the amount.

doubt
not to be sure, to question.

dock

dolphin

donkey

ABCDEFGHIJKLMNOPQRSTUVWXYZ

dough

dough
a soft mixture of flour and water.

dove
a kind of pigeon, often white.

down
1 lower; below.
2 soft hair or feathers.

doze
to sleep lightly.

dozen
12, twelve.

drag
to pull something along the ground.

dragon
in stories, a winged animal which breathes fire.

dragonfly
a long insect with fine wings.

drain
to take water away from something.

drains
the pipes which take the dirty water from buildings.

drama
1 stories that can be acted, plays.
2 an exciting happening.

draught
a cold stream of air entering a warmer room.

draughts
a game played with round pieces on a board with black and white squares.

draw
1 to make a picture with pencils or crayons, for example.
2 to pull.
3 to end a game with equal scores.

drawer
a box with handles and no top that fits closely into a piece of furniture.

dreadful
very bad, terrible.

dragonfly

draughts

draw

a b c **d** e f g h i j k l m n o p q r s t u v w x y z   61

dream

dream
    to see and hear things in your mind when you are asleep.

dress
    1 to put on your clothes.
    2 a woman's or girl's piece of clothing like a skirt and blouse together.
    3 to clean and cover a wound.

drift
    1 snow blown into a deep pile.
    2 to move aimlessly with the tide or with the wind.

drill
    1 a tool for making holes.
    2 to make a hole.
    3 exercises (for example, for soldiers).

drink
    to swallow liquids.

drip
    to fall in drops.

drive
    1 to make a vehicle, such as a car, or an animal move.
    2 a private road up to a house.

drizzle
    light rain falling gently.

drop
    1 one tiny spot of liquid.
    2 to fall from a height.

drought (rhymes with 'out')
    a long time when no rain falls and there is not enough water.

drown
    to die in water because you cannot breathe.

drug
    1 a substance used as a medicine.
    2 a substance used to make you feel different (for example, alcohol).

drum
    a musical instrument which is played by beating it with a stick.

dream

snowdrift

drip

dry

dry
   not wet or damp.

duck
   1 a common water bird.
   2 to bend down quickly (for example, so as not to be hit).

duel
   a fight between two people armed with the same sort of weapons.

duet
   a song or a piece of music for two people.

dull
   1 not bright.
   2 not interesting.

dumb
   unable to speak.

dump
   1 a place where things are stored roughly or thrown away.
   2 to put something down heavily or carelessly.

dungeon
   a prison below the ground.

dust
   tiny specks of dirt.

duster
   a cloth to remove dust.

duty
   something that you should do.

duvet (say 'doovay')
   a padded bed cover, used instead of sheets and blankets.

dwarf
   a person or animal much smaller than usual.

dwell
   to live in a certain place.

dye
   to make something a certain colour by placing it in a special liquid.

duck

dungeon

duster

Ee

each
    every one by itself.

eager
    very keen.

eagle
    a kind of large, wild bird which kills small animals for food.

ear
    1 the part of the head with which you hear.
    2 where the seed is found in the corn plant.

early
    1 before the time fixed.
    2 near the beginning.

earn
    1 to get something by working (money, for example).
    2 to deserve.

earth
    1 the world in which we live.
    2 the soil in which things grow.

earthquake
    when the earth's surface shakes.

earwig
    a kind of small insect.

east
    the direction from which the sun rises.

easy
    simple to do, not difficult to understand.

eat
    to bite, chew and swallow food.

echo
    the same sound which comes back to you in an empty place.

edge
    the rim, the border.

eagle

Earth

eat

ABCDEFGHIJKLMNOPQRSTUVWXYZ

editor

editor
1 the person in charge of a newspaper or magazine.
2 a person who prepares a book or a newspaper for printing.

education
learning and teaching, especially in schools, colleges and universities.

eel
a kind of fish which looks like a snake.

effort
the use of all your strength or ability in trying to do something.

egg
the rounded object from which some creatures (for example, fish and birds) are hatched.

either
one or the other (of two people or things).

elastic
a material that will stretch and then go back to its own length.

elbow
the joint in the middle of the arm.

elder
1 the older one of two people.
2 a kind of tree with white flowers and black berries.

election
choosing someone by a vote.

electricity
a power for heating, lighting or driving things, which goes through wires.

elephant
a very large animal with a trunk and two tusks, found in Africa and India.

elm
a kind of large tree.

embarrass
to make someone feel uncomfortable.

embrace
to put your arms round someone lovingly, to hug.

eel

elephant

embrace

a b c d e f g h i j k l m n o p q r s t u v w x y z   65

embroider

embroider
  to sew patterns on cloth.
emerald
  1 a bright-green precious stone.
  2 the colour of this precious stone.
emergency
  something very bad which needs to be dealt with right away.
emotion
  something you feel strongly, such as anger or love.
emperor
  a man who is the head of a number of countries.
empire
  many countries which are all under the same ruler.
employ
  to give paid work to someone.
empress
  a woman who is the head of a number of countries; the wife of an emperor.
empty
  with nothing at all inside.
enamel
  1 a special kind of hard, shiny paint.
  2 the hard covering on your teeth.
encourage
  to act or speak in a way which helps someone to do something.
encyclopedia
  a book containing facts about a lot of different things.
end
  1 the last part of something.
  2 to finish.
enemy
  someone you fight against.
energy
  power, strength to do things.
engine
  a machine driven by some sort of power which makes things move.

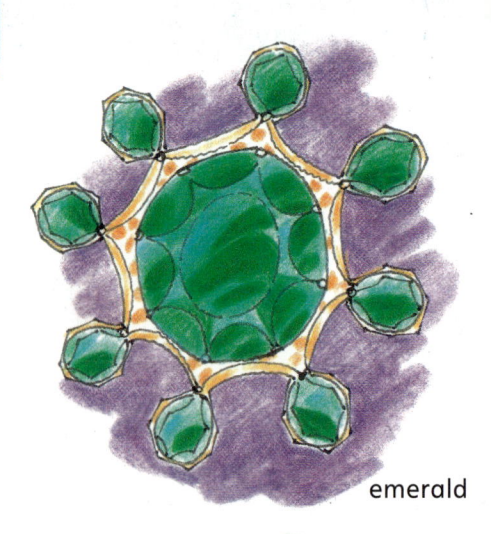

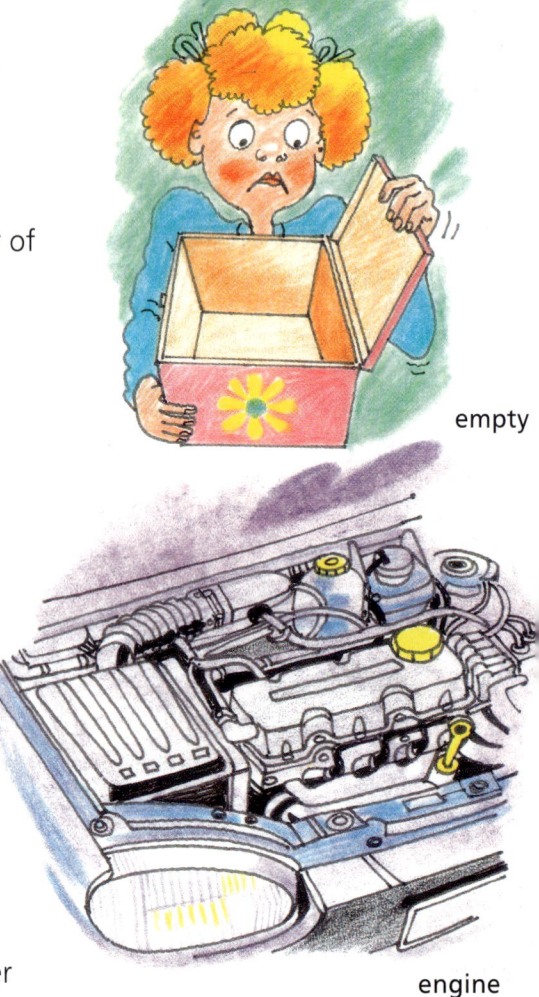

emerald

empty

engine

engineer

engineer
someone who plans or looks after machines, roads or bridges, for example.

enjoy
to like doing something very much.

enormous
very large.

enough
as many or as much as needed.

enter
to go into or to come into.

entertain
to put people in a good mood by amusing them.

entertainment
something which is done to give pleasure to people.

enthusiastic
very keen, very interested.

entrance
the place where you enter, the way in.

entry
1 going or coming in.
2 an entrance.

envelope
the paper cover in which a letter is placed.

envy
to wish you could have what somebody else has.

equal
1 exactly the same as.
2 just as good as.

equator
an imaginary line round the earth halfway between the North and South Poles.

equipment
the things you need to do something.

errand
a short journey to take a message or to fetch something.

error
a mistake.

entrance

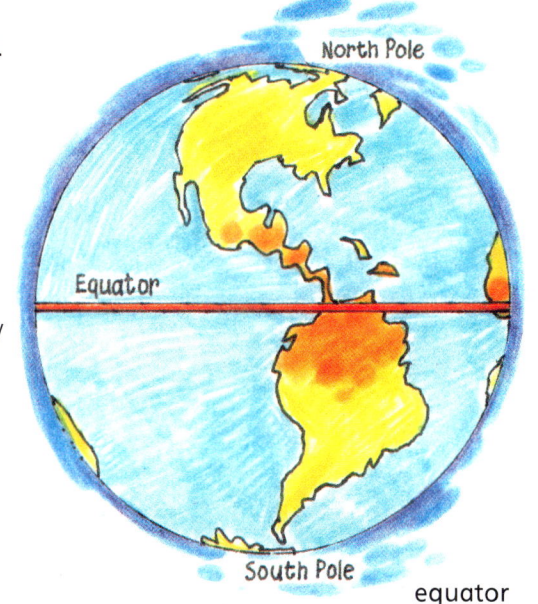

envelope

equator

a b c d e f g h i j k l m n o p q r s t u v w x y z   67

escape

escape
to get away, to find a way out.

especially
very, more than usual.

estate
1 a large piece of land belonging to one person.
2 a number of houses and shops built in one place.

estimate
to guess the size or price of something.

even
1 flat and smooth.
2 (of a number) that can be divided by two, not odd.

evening
the time between afternoon and night.

event
1 a happening, especially an important one.
2 an item on a sports programme.

ever
always, at all times.

evergreen
a plant that does not lose its leaves in the winter.

every
each one of many.

evil
very bad, very wicked.

exact
absolutely correct, quite right.

exaggerate
to say more than is really true.

examination
a test of how good someone or something is, a check.

examine
to look at something carefully.

example
1 one thing taken out of a number of things to show what the rest are like.
2 good behaviour you should copy.

escape

evergreen

examine

ABCDEFGHIJKLMNOPQRSTUVWXYZ

excellent

excellent
very good.
exchange
to change for something else.
excite
to give strong and often pleasant feelings.
excuse (rhymes with 'loose')
a reason for not doing what you should have done.
excuse (rhymes with 'news')
to forgive.
execute
to put to death.
exercise
movement such as walking or running to keep you fit.
exhibition
a display, a show (of pictures, for example).
exit
the way out of a place.
expand
to grow larger, to spread out.
expect
to think something will happen.
expedition
a special journey to a place to find out more about it.
expensive
costing a lot of money.
experiment
a test done on something to find out more about it.
expert
a person who is very good at something or knows a lot about something.
explain
to say clearly how something happened or what something is about.
explode
to burst or blow up with a loud noise.

exercise

exhibition

exit

a b c d e f g h i j k l m n o p q r s t u v w x y z

explore

explore
   to search a place thoroughly to find out more about it.

export
   to send goods out of a country.

express
   1 to state clearly.
   2 travelling more quickly than usual (for example, an **express train**).

extra
   1 in addition to.
   2 more than is needed or usual.

extraordinary
   very strange, unusual.

eye
   1 the part of the head with which you see.
   2 the hole in a needle.

express

extra

retina
optic nerve
muscles
iris
lens
pupil

pupil
iris
eye

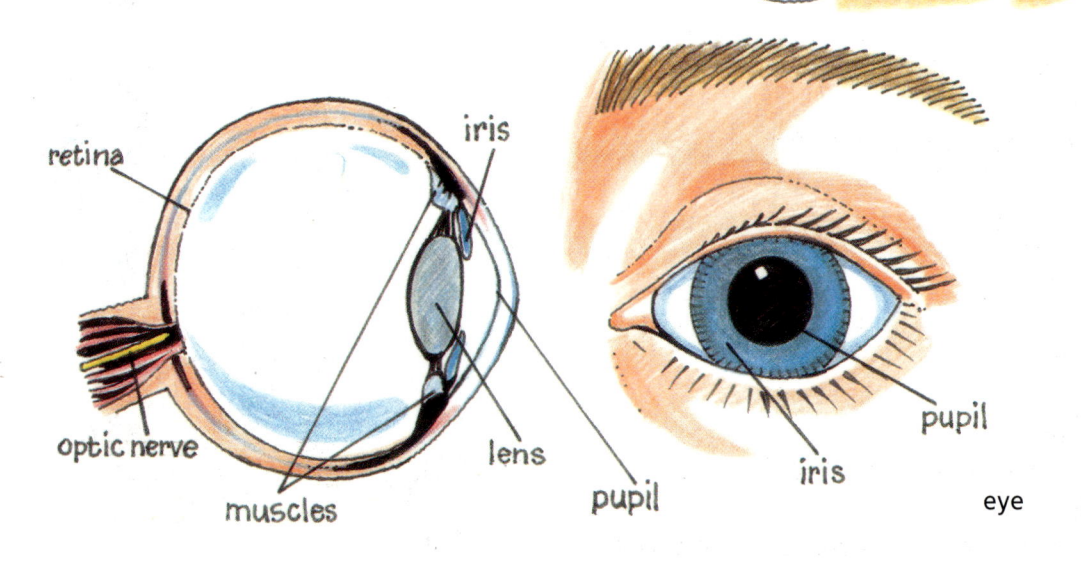

70   A B C D **E** F G H I J K L M N O P Q R S T U V W X Y Z

Ff

fable
　a story or legend, often about animals, which teaches you something.

face
　1 the front part of the head.
　2 the front of an object.
　3 to turn towards something.

fact
　something that is true.

factory
　a place where things are made by machinery.

factory

fade
　1 to lose colour, to become dim.
　2 to begin to grow weaker.

fail
　1 not to do something that you are expected to do.
　2 not to pass an exam.

faint
　1 not clear, not easy to see.
　2 to lose one's senses, stop being conscious.

fair

fair
　1 light in colour, not dark, blonde.
　2 reasonable, just.
　3 an open-air entertainment; a market.
　4 neither good nor bad, quite good.

fairy
　an imaginary person with magic power.

faith
　belief in somebody or something.

faithful
　true; able to be trusted.

fall
　to drop, come down; to become lower.

fall

abcde**f**ghijklmnopqrstuvwxyz　71

false

false
 1 not true; not real.
 2 not able to be trusted.

familiar
 well-known to you.

family
 a group of close relations, especially a father, a mother and their children.

famine
 being without food for a very long time.

famous
 well-known because of what you have done.

fan
 1 an instrument to make air move and keep you cool.
 2 a person who takes a great interest (in a football team or a pop singer, for example).

fancy
 1 to think that you can see something.
 2 decorated, not plain.
 3 to want.

fang
 a long, sharp tooth on some animals and snakes.

far
 not near, a long way away.

fare
 money paid for a journey.

farm
 land used for growing crops and keeping animals.

farmer
 a person who owns or looks after a farm.

fashion
 up-to-date dress and style.

fast
 1 very quick, at great speed.
 2 a time without food.
 3 stopped from moving.

fasten
 to tie or join things together.

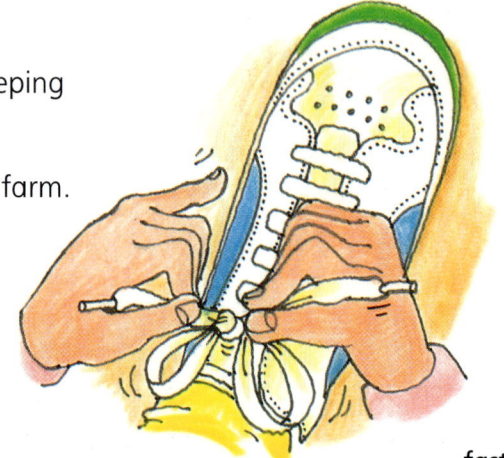

fans

farm

fasten

ABCDE**F**GHIJKLMNOPQRSTUVWXYZ

fat

fat
 1 very big all round, not thin.
 2 the greasy part of meat.

fatal
 causing death.

father
 a male parent.

fault
 1 something which is not right and which spoils a thing or person.
 2 a mistake, something you do wrong.

favour
 something good you do for someone.

favourite
 the one that you like better than any of the others.

fawn
 1 a young deer.
 2 a light-brown colour.

fax
 to send a printed message or picture through a machine which uses a telephone line.

fear
 to be afraid of; to be frightened that something might happen.

feast
 a large, special meal; a banquet.

feather
 one of the flat, light parts which cover a bird's body and wings.

feeble
 weak, with no strength.

feed
 to give food to.

feel
 1 to know something by touching it.
 2 to think.

fellow
 a man or boy, a person.

female
 a girl or a woman; an animal which can be a mother.

fawn

fax

feather

a b c d e **f** g h i j k l m n o p q r s t u v w x y z   73

feminine

feminine
concerning girls or women.

fence
1 something built of wood or metal to separate one place from another.
2 to fight with swords as a sport.

fern
a plant with feathery leaves but no flowers.

ferret
a small, furry animal used for hunting rabbits.

ferry
a boat which carries people and vehicles across water.

festival
a special occasion for large numbers of people to enjoy themselves.

fetch
to go and get, to bring back what you were sent for.

fever
an illness which makes the body hot.

few
not many.

fiddle
a violin.

fidget
to be restless; to wriggle about.

field
a piece of land with a hedge, fence or wall around it.

fierce
violent, angry, cruel.

fight
a struggle or battle between two or more people.

figure
1 a number used in mathematics.
2 a shape, especially of the human body.

ferry

fetch

fierce

ABCDE**F**GHIJKLMNOPQRSTUVWXYZ

file

file
1 an instrument with a rough edge for making things smooth.
2 a line of people one behind the other.
3 a box or folder for keeping papers in an office.

fill
to make full.

film
1 a very thin covering.
2 a roll put into a camera to take photographs.
3 a story shown in a cinema or on television.

filthy
very dirty.

fin
one of the thin, flat parts of a fish which help it to swim.

final
1 the end, the last.
2 the last match in a competition, which decides the winner.

find
to come across something you have been looking for.

fine
1 when the weather is pleasant.
2 very good, excellent.
3 a sum of money paid as a punishment for breaking the law.

finger
one of the five long parts of the hand.

finish
to complete, to end.

fir
a kind of evergreen tree with cones.

fire
1 things burning.
2 to shoot a gun.

fire-fighter
a person whose job it is to prevent or put out fires.

filthy

finish

fire-fighter

a b c d e f g h i j k l m n o p q r s t u v w x y z   75

firework

firework
a container with gunpowder in it which makes a display of coloured flames and sparks when lit.

firm
1 without changing; fixed.
2 a group of people running a business.

first
1 at the very beginning.
2 coming before everyone else (in a race, for example).

first aid
giving help to someone who is injured or ill before a doctor comes.

fish
1 an animal which lives and breathes in water.
2 to try to catch fish.

fisherman
a person who catches fish.

fist
the hand and fingers closed tightly together.

fit
1 in good health, well and strong.
2 suitable.
3 to be the right size for.

fix
1 to put in place firmly.
2 to put right.

fizzy
with a lot of bubbles.

flag
a piece of cloth with a special pattern and colours (the sign of a country or club, for example).

flake
a small, thin piece of something.

flame
the bright, blazing part of a fire.

firework

first

flags

flap

flap
1 a piece that hangs down or over something.
2 to move something flat up and down (a bird's wings, for example).

flash
a beam of light which comes and goes quickly.

flask
a container for keeping things hot or cold.

flat
1 level.
2 a set of rooms all on one floor.
3 below the correct note in music.

flavour
the taste of something.

flea
a tiny jumping insect which bites people and animals.

flee
to go away quickly; to run from trouble or danger.

fleet
a number of ships together.

flesh
the soft part of the body which covers the bones.

flight
1 flying.
2 escaping.

fling
to throw something away from you.

float
to stay on the surface of water without sinking.

flock
a number of animals of the same sort together.

flood
when water overflows (from a river, for example).

floor
the part of a room you walk on.

flask

flock

flood

abcde**f**ghijklmnopqrstuvwxyz 77

flour

flour
: wheat which has been crushed into a powder which is used for baking.

flow
: to move smoothly along like running water.

flower
: the part of a plant, usually colourful, which produces the seeds.

flu
: an illness like a very bad cold which causes shivering and aches all over the body.

fluff
: tiny, soft pieces of cloth, for example, which are blown about and catch dust.

flute
: a kind of high-pitched wood or metal musical instrument played by blowing.

flutter
: the quick movement of a bird's wings, for example.

fly
: 1 to move through the air, especially on wings or in an aircraft.
: 2 a kind of small insect with wings.

foal
: a young horse.

foam
: bubbles on the top of a liquid.

fog
: air which is thick with mist and smoke.

fold
: to bend something so that one part covers another.

folder
: a cardboard cover (for papers, for example).

folk
: people.

follow
: to go after; to come after.

fond
: **to be fond of somebody** to like them very much.

flute

fly

fold

ABCDEFGHIJKLMNOPQRSTUVWXYZ

food

food
what you eat and drink to keep you alive and make you grow.

fool
1 a person who behaves in a silly way.
2 to trick somebody.

foolish
slightly stupid, silly.

foot
1 the part of the leg you stand on.
2 a measure of length.

forbid
to tell somebody not to do something.

force
1 strength, power.
2 to make somebody do something.

forecast
to say what is likely to happen.

forehead
the part of the head between the hair and the eyes.

foreign
belonging to another country.

forest
a large area of woodland.

forge
1 to copy someone's writing, painting or signature, usually for a bad reason.
2 a blacksmith's workshop.

forget
1 not to remember.
2 to leave something behind.

fork
1 a small tool with long, thin spikes for eating with.
2 a large tool with long, thin spikes for digging and lifting things.
3 where two roads or rivers meet.

form
1 the shape of something.
2 a printed paper with spaces for you to write things in.
3 a class in a school.

foot

forehead

fork

a b c d e **f** g h i j k l m n o p q r s t u v w x y z   79

fort

fort
    a building with high, strong walls to keep out enemies.

fortnight
    a period of two weeks.

fortunate
    lucky.

fortune
    1 good or bad luck.
    2 a lot of money.

forward
    towards the front.

fossil
    the mark or remains of a creature or plant found in rocks.

foster
    to bring up a child who is not your own.

foul
    1 very dirty or bad.
    2 something that is against the rules (for example, in a sport).

fox
    a wild animal like a dog with a reddish-brown coat and a long, thick tail.

frame
    a border placed round a picture.

freckle
    one of the tiny, light-brown marks found on the skin of some people.

free
    1 able to do as you wish.
    2 given away for nothing.

freeze
    to make or be very hard and cold; to turn into ice.

frequent
    happening often.

fresh
    1 new; newly gathered; just made.
    2 not tired.
    3 **fresh water** not salty (in rivers and lakes, for example).

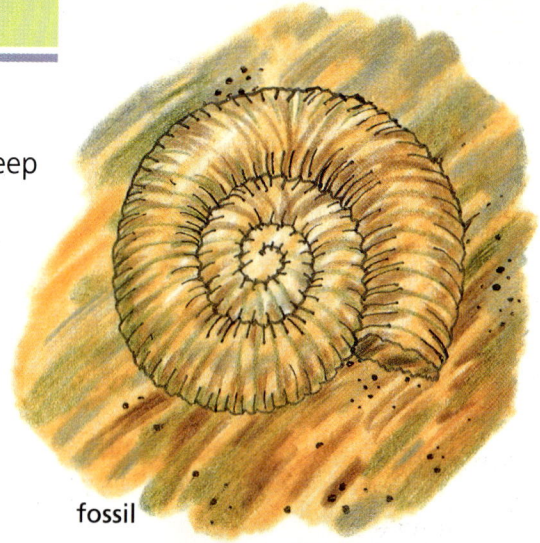

fossil

fox

frame

ABCDEFGHIJKLMNOPQRSTUVWXYZ

fridge

fridge
short for **refrigerator**.

friend
somebody you like and can trust and like doing things with.

fright
sudden fear.

frill
a decoration round the edge.

fringe
1 short hair brushed forward over the forehead.
2 a border of loose threads (used to decorate a rug or a lampshade, for example).

frisky
lively, jumping with pleasure.

frock
a dress.

frog
a small, jumping animal which can live on land and in water.

front
the part opposite the back, the beginning of something.

frost
1 white, powdery ice seen in very cold weather.
2 very cold, freezing weather.

froth
bubbles on top of a liquid, foam.

frown
to wrinkle the forehead to show you are annoyed or puzzled.

frozen
very cold; made into ice.

fruit
the part of certain plants where the seeds are found; many kinds are good to eat (for example, strawberries, oranges).

fry
to cook in hot fat or oil in a pan.

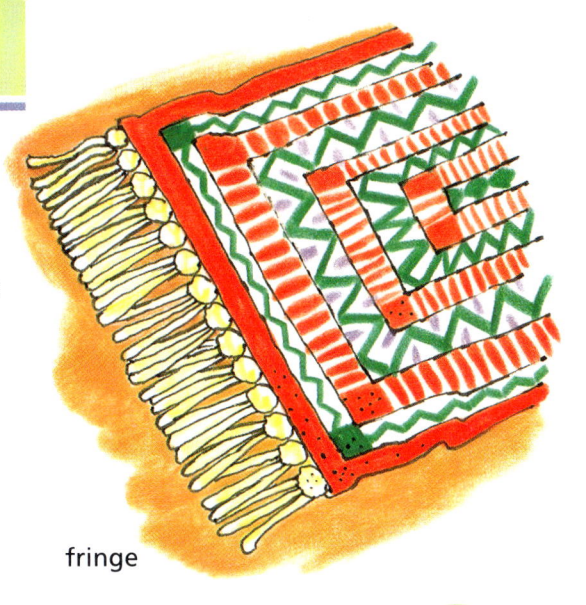

fringe

frog

frown

fudge

fudge
a kind of soft, brown toffee.

fuel
anything that can be burned to give heat or light.

full
unable to hold any more.

fun
something enjoyable, amusement, lively pleasure.

fund
a collection of money for something special.

funeral
the ceremony held when someone dies.

funnel
1 the chimney on a ship or an engine.
2 a tube with a wide mouth (used to pour liquids into bottles, for example).

funny
1 amusing, making you laugh.
2 strange, odd.

fur
the soft, hairy covering of some animals.

furious
very angry.

furniture
chairs, tables and similar things.

fuse
1 a piece of material which is lit to set off an explosion or a firework.
2 part of an electric plug or system.

fuss
an excited state, usually about something quite small.

future
the time yet to come.

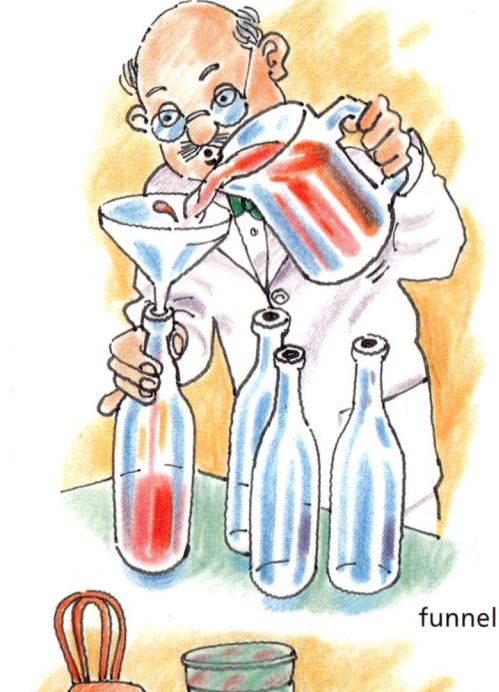

full

funnel

furniture

Gg

gain
1 a profit that is made.
2 to get or win something.

gale
a very strong wind.

galleon
(long ago) a kind of large sailing ship.

gallery
1 a high platform, often with seats, in a cinema, a theatre or a church.
2 a building or a large room used for showing paintings or sculptures.

galley
1 a ship's kitchen.
2 (long ago) a kind of low sailing ship with many oars.

gallon
a measure of liquid.

gallop
to move very fast on four legs like a horse.

gamble
to play games for money.

game
1 something that you play; a sport.
2 wild animals or birds which are hunted for sport or food.

gander
a male goose.

gang
a group of people doing something together.

gaol (say 'jail')
a prison.

gap
an opening between two places or things.

garage
a place where cars are kept or repaired.

gale

galleon

garage

a b c d e f **g** h i j k l m n o p q r s t u v w x y z   83

garden

garden
    land where flowers, fruit and vegetables are grown.

gas
    1 something which is neither liquid nor solid (for example, air).
    2 a kind of gas which burns, used for heating and cooking.

gasp
    to breathe in very quickly, often in surprise.

gate
    a kind of door in a wall or fence.

gather
    1 to collect together.
    2 to pick flowers or other plants.

gay
    happy, cheerful.

gaze
    to look for a long time; to stare steadily.

gazelle
    a kind of small deer found in Africa and Asia.

gear
    1 a set of wheels with teeth to make an engine turn.
    2 what you need with you (to play some sports, for example).

gem
    a stone, like a diamond or a pearl, which is very valuable.

general
    1 usual; often done.
    2 an army officer of high rank.

generous
    kind; giving away freely.

gentle
    soft, not rough; quiet and kind.

gentleman
    1 a man who is well-mannered.
    2 a polite word for a man.

genuine
    real, true.

garden

gazelle

gears

geography

geography
   knowledge about the earth and its people.

gerbil
   a desert animal like a small rat, often kept as a pet.

germ
   a tiny living thing in the blood that can cause illness.

ghost
   the spirit of a dead person, believed to be seen moving about.

giant
   1 a huge man (in a fairy story, for example).
   2 anything that is much larger than usual.

giddy
   dizzy, when everything seems to be going round and round.

gift
   a present.

giggle
   to laugh in a foolish way.

gills
   the opening in a fish's head by which it breathes.

ginger
   1 a kind of hot-tasting flavouring used in cooking.
   2 a reddish-brown colour.

giraffe
   an African wild animal with a very long neck and long legs.

girl
   1 a female child.
   2 a young woman.

give
   to hand over to someone else.

glad
   happy, pleased, delighted.

glance
   to look at something and then look away quickly.

gerbil

gift

giraffe

a b c d e f **g** h i j k l m n o p q r s t u v w x y z 85

glare

glare
 1 to stare at in anger.
 2 unpleasant brightness.

glass
 1 a hard material through which you can usually see.
 2 a cup which has no handle and is made of glass.

glasses
 two pieces of glass or plastic put in a light frame, worn to help you to see better.

gleam
 to shine faintly.

glide
 to move along very smoothly.

glider
 a kind of aeroplane that glides through the air without an engine.

glimpse
 a very short look, a glance.

glitter
 to throw out bright rays of light, to sparkle.

globe
 1 an round object like a ball.
 2 a round ball with a map of the world drawn on it.

gloomy
 1 dark and dismal.
 2 sad and serious.

glove
 a covering for the hand with a separate place for each finger.

glow
 to shine with a soft light, to burn without flame.

glue
 something used to stick things together.

gnome (say 'nome')
 a dwarf or goblin that is supposed to live under the ground.

go
 to move away; to leave.

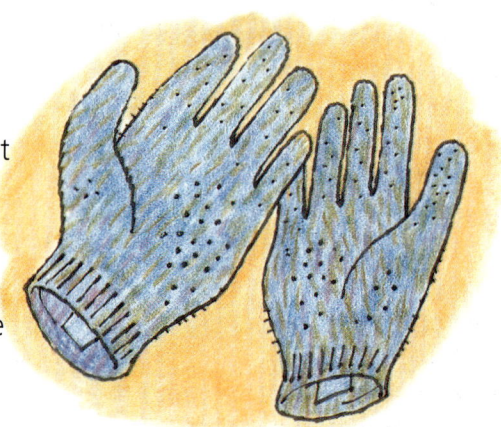

glasses

globe

gloves

ABCDEF**G**HIJKLMNOPQRSTUVWXYZ

goal

goal
1 a place you aim at in games such as football and hockey.
2 the score made when the ball goes into goal.

goat
a kind of animal which has horns, sometimes kept on farms for its milk.

gobble
to eat greedily and noisily.

goblin
a kind of wicked fairy.

God
the being who is above all others and to whom people pray.

gold
a yellow precious metal.

golden
1 looking like gold.
2 made of gold.

goldfish
a small, orange fish often kept as a pet.

golf
a game played on a large stretch of land with special clubs and a small ball.

good
1 right; true.
2 kind.
3 well-behaved.

goodbye
something said when leaving people.

goods
things which are bought, sold and owned.

goose
a bird like a large duck.

gooseberry
a green fruit which grows on a small, prickly bush.

gorgeous
splendid, magnificent, very beautiful.

gorilla
the largest kind of ape.

goal

goat

goose

a b c d e f **g** h i j k l m n o p q r s t u v w x y z 87

gossip

gossip
1 to talk for a long time about unimportant things, often about other people.
2 a person who tells usually hurtful stories about other people.

govern
to be in control of, to rule over (a country, for example).

government
the people who are in charge of a country.

gown
a dress.

grab
to snatch, to grasp quickly.

grab

grace
1 a short prayer before or after a meal.
2 a beautiful way of moving.

gradual
little by little.

grain
1 a tiny piece of sand or soil.
2 the seed of a cereal plant, used for food.
3 the lines in wood.

gram
a small unit of mass; 1000 of these are equal to a kilogram.

grand
very large and fine.

grandfather, grandpa, grandad
the father of your father or mother.

grandmother, grandma, granny
the mother of your father or mother.

granite
a very hard rock often used for buildings and monuments.

grape
a small, juicy fruit with green or purple skin.

grapes

grapefruit
a sour, yellow fruit like a large orange.

grapefruit

ABCDEF**G**HIJKLMNOPQRSTUVWXYZ

grasp

grasp
   1 to hold firmly in the hand.
   2 to understand what you have been told.

grass
   the common green plant grown in fields and gardens.

grasshopper
   a kind of insect with strong back legs for jumping.

grate
   1 to rub something into little pieces using a rough surface.
   2 where the fire burns in a fireplace.

grateful
   thankful, feeling gratitude.

grave
   1 a burial place in the ground.
   2 serious.

gravel
   small pieces of stone.

gravity
   the force which pulls objects towards the earth.

gravy
   a brown liquid eaten with meat, often made from the juice of the meat.

graze
   1 to rub away the skin.
   2 to feed from grass.

grease
   1 animal fat.
   2 thick oil used to make machinery run smoothly.

great
   1 big.
   2 important.
   3 very good.

greedy
   always wanting more; never satisfied.

green
   1 the colour of grass.
   2 an area of grass.

grate

gravy

graze

a b c d e f **g** h i j k l m n o p q r s t u v w x y z

greenhouse

greenhouse
a building with glass walls and roof in which plants are grown.

greet
to welcome with words and actions.

grey
a colour halfway between black and white.

grief
sorrow, deep sadness.

grill
a part of a cooker using overhead direct heat.

grim
stern; severe; fierce.

grin
a wide smile.

grind
1 to rub something until it becomes powder.
2 to sharpen (a tool, for example) by rubbing the edge.

grip
to grasp tightly.

groan
to make a low, sad sound, usually when hurt.

grocer
a person who sells foods and other goods for the house.

ground
1 the surface of the earth; land.
2 a place for playing certain outdoor games.

group
a number of people, animals or things together.

grow
1 to become bigger.
2 to raise plants.

growl
to make a noise like an angry dog, for example.

greenhouse

grill

grin

grub

grub
an insect, such as a caterpillar, before it has grown wings or legs.

grubby
dirty.

gruff
having a rough, coarse voice or manner.

grumble
to complain, not loudly but often.

grunt
a noise like that made by a pig.

guard
1 to keep safe.
2 a person whose job it is to protect something or someone.
3 a person in charge of a train on its journey.

guard

guardian
someone who looks after another person, especially when taking the place of a parent.

guess
to say what you think is correct without really knowing.

guest
1 a visitor to someone's house.
2 a person staying in a hotel.

guide
a person who shows the way.

guitars

guilt
1 having done wrong.
2 the feeling of having done wrong.

guitar
a musical instrument with six strings, played by plucking the strings.

gull
a kind of common seabird.

gulp
to swallow greedily and noisily.

gull

a b c d e f g h i j k l m n o p q r s t u v w x y z

gum

gum
1 something used to stick things together.
2 the part of the mouth round the roots of the teeth.
3 chewing gum; a chewy sweet.

gun
a weapon from which bullets are fired.

gurgle
to make a bubbling noise like water leaving a container.

gush
to flow out quickly in large amounts.

gust
a sudden wind.

gutter
a channel for water (along the edge of a road or roof, for example).

guy
1 a model of Guy Fawkes, burnt on a bonfire on 5 November.
2 a man.

gymnastics
exercises for the body.

gypsy
a member of a tribe of wandering people.

gush

gutter

gymnastics

Hh

habit
　something you do a lot without thinking about it much, a custom.

haddock
　a kind of sea-fish used as food.

hail
　1 frozen raindrops.
　2 to call to someone, to greet.

hair
　thread-like strands which grow on the head and skin.

hairdresser
　a person who cuts and arranges hair.

half
　one of two equal parts of a thing.

hall
　1 a very large room for meetings.
　2 an entrance passage.
　3 a very large house.

halo
　1 a circle painted or drawn round the heads of holy people in pictures.
　2 a ring of light round the sun or moon.

halt
　to stop.

ham
　salted or smoked meat from a pig's leg.

hamburger
　a round, flat cake of minced meat fried and eaten in a roll.

hammer
　a tool with a metal head used to drive in nails.

hammock
　a hanging mattress or bed held up by ropes.

halo

hammer

hammock

a b c d e f g h i j k l m n o p q r s t u v w x y z　93

hamper

hamper
1 a large basket with a lid.
2 to hinder.

hamster
a small animal like a large mouse, often kept as a pet.

hand
1 the part of the arm below the wrist.
2 a pointer on a clock.
3 to pass something to someone.

handbag
a bag carried in the hand.

handicap
something that keeps you back; a disadvantage.

handicapped
having something badly wrong with you (for example, not being able to walk).

handkerchief
a small piece of cloth for wiping the nose.

handle
1 to touch with the hand.
2 the part of something which you hold in your hand.

handlebars
the part of a bicycle you hold on to to steer it.

handsome
good-looking.

handy
useful.

hang
to fasten something at the top so that it falls loose (from a hook or nail, for example).

happen
to take place.

happy
feeling very pleased, glad.

harbour
a place of shelter for boats.

hard
1 difficult to do.
2 tough, firm, not soft.

hamper

handkerchief

handle

A B C D E F G **H** I J K L M N O P Q R S T U V W X Y Z

hardy

hardy
1 strong, able to bear cold or pain, for example.
2 (of a plant) able to live in difficult conditions.

hare
an animal like a large rabbit.

harm
danger; trouble.

harness
the straps used to control an animal.

harp
a musical instrument which rests on the floor and is played by plucking strings.

harsh
rough, severe, unkind.

harvest
1 a crop of food to be gathered in.
2 the time when this is done.

haste
speed, quickness, hurry.

hat
a covering worn on the head.

hatch
1 to be born from an egg.
2 to make secret plans.
3 an opening in the floor (the deck of a ship, for example).

hate
to dislike very much.

haul
to drag, to pull with effort.

haunted
often visited by a ghost.

hawk
a large bird which hunts small birds or animals for food.

hay
dried grass used as animal food.

hazel
1 a small tree with brown nuts which you can eat.
2 a light-brown colour.

harp

harvest

hawk

a b c d e f g h i j k l m n o p q r s t u v w x y z   95

head

head
1 the part of the body above the neck.
2 the chief person.
3 the front part or top of something.

headache
a pain in the head.

heal
to make well again after being hurt or ill, to cure.

health
1 the state of your body or mind.
2 freedom from illness, fitness.

heap
things placed one on top of another untidily, a pile.

heap

hear
to catch the sound of; to listen to.

heart
1 the part of the body which pumps the blood round it.
2 the centre or most important part of something.
3 a shape with two rounded parts at the top and a sharp point at the bottom.
4 a playing card with red heart shapes on it.

heat
1 warmth, being hot.
2 one of the races leading to a final.

heave

heather
a small plant which has purple or white flowers and grows on moorlands.

heave
1 to pull strongly.
2 to lift something and then throw it.

heaven
the place where God is said to live; perfect happiness.

heavy
having great weight, not easily lifted.

hedge
small bushes or trees grown in lines to separate fields or gardens.

hedge

ABCDEFGHIJKLMNOPQRSTUVWXYZ

hedgehog

hedgehog
a small animal with prickles on its back which rolls itself into a ball when in danger.

heel
the back part of the foot.

height
the distance from top to bottom, how tall something or someone is.

helicopter
an aircraft which flies by means of a large overhead propeller and can lift straight up into the air.

hell
the place where the Devil is said to live; a place of very great suffering.

helmet
a covering to protect the head.

help
to do something for another person, to assist.

helpless
unable to do something for yourself, needing the help of others.

hem
an edge of cloth which has been turned over and stitched.

hen
1 a kind of bird kept on a farm. Its eggs and meat are used for food.
2 a female bird.

herb
a plant used as a medicine or for its flavour.

herd
a large number of the same kind of animals together.

hermit
a person who lives on his or her own, usually in a lonely place.

hedgehog

helmet

herd

a b c d e f g **h** i j k l m n o p q r s t u v w x y z

hero

hero
1 a man or boy who acts with great bravery.
2 the main man or boy in a story, for example.

heroine
1 a woman or girl who acts with great bravery.
2 the main woman or girl in a story, for example.

herring
a kind of sea-fish used for food.

hibernate
to sleep through the winter as some animals do.

hiccup
a sudden noise in your throat, usually because you have eaten or drunk too quickly.

hide
1 to keep in a secret place.
2 to go where you cannot be found.
3 the skin of an animal.

hideous
terrible to look at, ugly, frightening.

high
1 tall, well above the ground.
2 great.
3 (of a sound) the opposite of low.

highwayman
(long ago) a man who stopped travellers and robbed them.

hill
a high piece of land often with steep sides.

hinge
a moving joint which allows a door or window to open and close easily.

hint
to say something in a roundabout way; to suggest.

hip
the place where the legs join the body.

hibernate

high

hinge

hippopotamus

hippopotamus
a kind of large African animal which lives near water.

hire
to borrow something for a short time and pay for its use.

hiss
to push air sharply through the teeth.

history
what happened in the past.

hit
to strike or knock something or someone.

hive
where bees live.

hoarse
having a rough, harsh voice.

hobby
something you like doing in your spare time.

hockey
a game played by two teams with curved sticks and a ball.

hoe
a tool used for breaking up the soil and taking out weeds.

hold
1 to keep a grip of.
2 to have inside.
3 the storage part of a ship.

hole
an opening; a gap.

holiday
a time of rest and enjoyment; a time when you are free from work or school.

hollow
empty, with nothing inside.

holly
an evergreen bush with sharp, pointed leaves and red berries.

holy
connected with God and religion.

hippopotamus

hive

holiday

a b c d e f g **h** i j k l m n o p q r s t u v w x y z

home

home
the place where you live.

honest
able to be trusted, truthful.

honey
a sweet food made by bees.

hood
1 a covering to protect the head and neck.
2 a folding cover for a baby's pram or a car.

hoof
the hard part of the foot of some animals (horses, for example).

hook
a bent and pointed piece of metal, wood or plastic to hold or catch things.

hoop
a ring of wood, metal or plastic.

hoot
1 the sound made by a car horn, for example.
2 the sound made by an owl.

hop
to jump up and down on one foot.

hope
to wish and believe that something pleasant will happen.

hopeless
1 giving no reason for hope.
2 very bad.

horizon
the line where the sky and the earth seem to touch.

horn
1 one of the two sharp bones which grow out of the head of some animals.
2 a kind of musical instrument you blow through.
3 an instrument on a car or bus which makes a noise to give a warning.

horrible
very unpleasant.

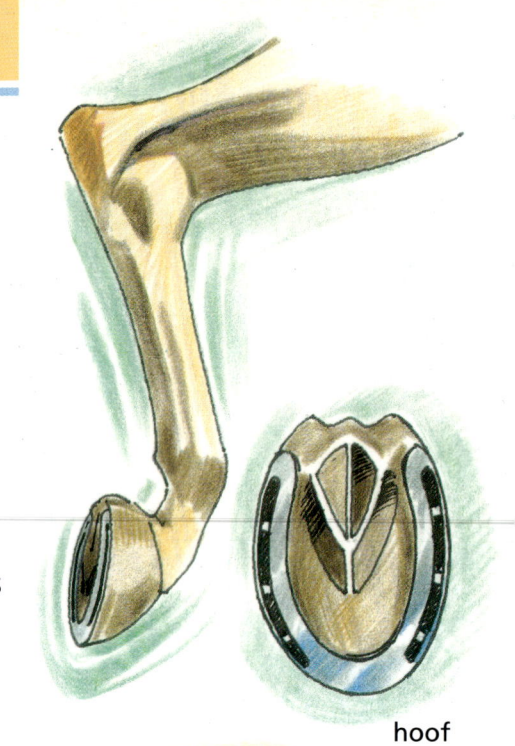

hoof

horizon

horn

horrid

horrid
  dreadful; causing fear.
horror
  something very frightening or terrible.
horse
  a large animal, with hooves and a mane, often used to ride on or to pull vehicles.
hose
  a tube through which water can be directed.
hospital
  a place where sick people are cared for.
hot
  very warm.
hotel
  a building where you can pay to stay the night.
hour
  a length of time equal to 60 minutes.
house
  a building in which people live.
hover
  to stay in the air above a place or thing.
howl
  a long, loud cry (like that made by a wolf, for example); a wailing noise.
hub
  the centre part of a wheel.
huff
  a bad mood.
hug
  to hold tightly in the arms.
huge
  very large.
hum
  1 the noise like that made by bees.
  2 to make the sound of a tune with the lips together.
human
  connected with people.
humble
  simple, modest, not proud.

hose

hospital

hover

a b c d e f g **h** i j k l m n o p q r s t u v w x y z

humour

humour
1 finding or making things funny.
2 a mood.

hump
a large lump on the back of a person or an animal.

hunger
a great need, usually for food.

hunt
1 to try to catch or kill wild animals.
2 to look very carefully for something.

hurl
to throw far away.

hurry
to move or do things very quickly; to rush.

hurt
to cause pain to, to injure, to damage.

husband
a married man.

hut
a small building, usually made of wood.

hyacinth
a kind of sweet-smelling spring flower grown from a bulb.

hyena
an African or Asian animal like a large dog which hunts other animals.

hymn
a religious song of praise or thanks.

humps

hyacinth.

hyena

ABCDEFG**H**IJKLMNOPQRSTUVWXYZ

Ii

ice
　frozen water.
iceberg
　a very large piece of ice floating in the sea.
ice cream
　a soft, sweet frozen food.
icicle
　a hanging spike of ice.
icing
　a sweet mixture sometimes spread over cakes and buns.
idea
　a thought, something in the mind.
ideal
　just what is needed, the best possible.
idiot
　a person who behaves stupidly.
idle
　not working; not wanting to work.
igloo
　a house made of snow blocks by Eskimos.
ignorant
　not wise, knowing nothing or very little.
ignore
　to pay no attention to, usually on purpose.
ill
　not well; sick.
ill-treat
　to treat badly.
illustrate
　to explain something by drawing pictures; to add pictures to.
imaginary
　not real, made up in the mind.
imitate
　to do the same as somebody else, to copy.

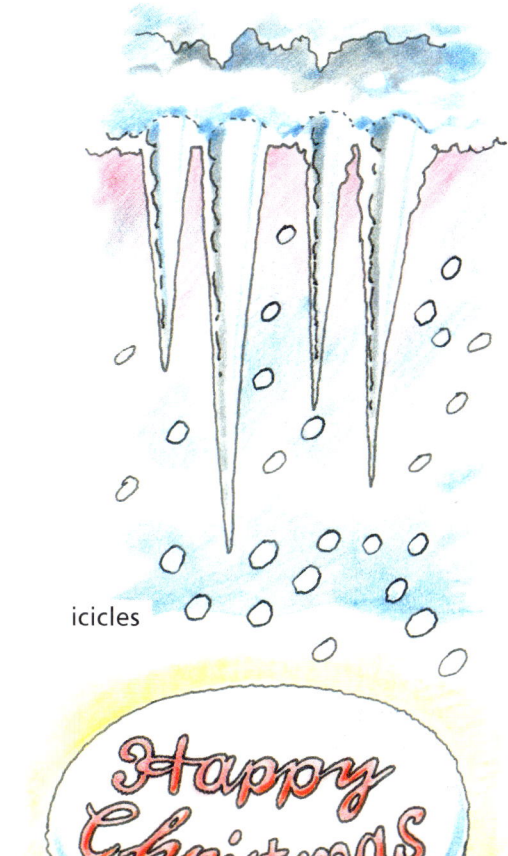

icicles

icing

imitate

a b c d e f g h **i** j k l m n o p q r s t u v w x y z　103

immediately

immediately
   at once.
important
   of great value, mattering very much.
impossible
   not able to be done, not possible.
improve
   to make something better; to get better.
inch
   a small measure of length.
include
   to put something in with other things.
income
   money which is earned or received.
increase
   to make larger or greater.
index
   a list showing what and where things can be found in a book.
individual
   a single person or thing.
infant
   a baby; a young child.
infectious
   (of an illness) likely to be passed on to someone else.
inform
   to tell; to give the news.
ingredient
   one of a number of things which together make up something else (in cooking, for example).
initial
   the first letter of a name.
injection
   the putting of medicine into the body with a special needle.
injure
   to hurt.
ink
   a coloured liquid used for writing or printing.

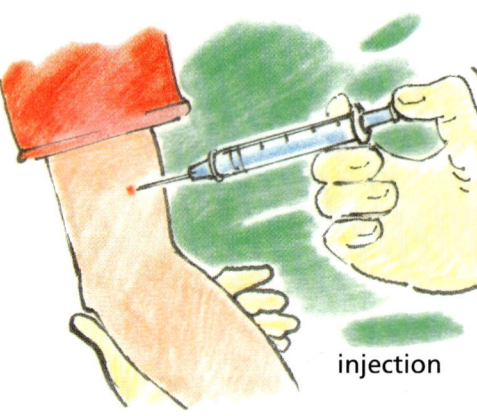

ingredients

injection

ink

inn

inn
　a place where people can buy a drink or a meal, a small hotel.

innocent
　not guilty; not at fault.

inquire
　to ask questions.

insane
　not in your right mind, mad.

insect
　a very small flying or crawling creature with six legs.

inside
　the part which is surrounded by something else; the part within.

instant
　1 a moment.
　2 made in a moment (for example, **instant coffee**).

instruct
　to teach someone how to do something.

instrument
　1 a tool.
　2 something on which music is played.

insult
　to be rude to someone by saying unkind things about them.

intelligent
　quick to learn, clever.

interesting
　worth knowing about.

interfere
　to get in the way of; to meddle.

interrupt
　to break into what other people are saying or doing.

interval
　a break, a pause; a space between things.

interview
　a meeting at which people ask and answer questions.

insect

instant coffee

instruments

a b c d e f g h i j k l m n o p q r s t u v w x y z　105

introduce

introduce
to make people known to each other.

invade
to enter, usually using force.

invent
to think of and make something for the first time.

inventor
someone who invents things.

invisible
not able to be seen.

invitation
asking someone to your house or to go somewhere with you.

invite
to ask somebody to come to your house, or to go somewhere with you.

iron
1 a hard, strong metal.
2 a tool for pressing clothes.

irritate
1 to make someone annoyed or angry.
2 to make something sore.

Islam
the religion of Muslims.

island
a piece of land with water all round it.

itch
a tickling of the skin that makes you want to scratch.

item
one thing out of a number of things.

ivory
the hard, white material elephants' tusks are made out of.

ivy
a climbing, evergreen plant.

invitation

iron

island

Jj

jab
   to poke at or to stab with something pointed.
jackal
   a wild animal that looks like a dog.
jacket
   a short coat.
jail
   a prison. The word may also be spelt **gaol**.
jam
   1 a food made from boiled fruit and sugar.
   2 to become fixed or difficult to move.
   3 a crowding together (of traffic, for example).
jar
   1 a container with a wide opening at the top.
   2 a movement or sound that makes you shudder.
jaw
   the bones to which teeth are fixed; the lower part of the face.
jazz
   a kind of modern music with a strong rhythm.
jealous
   wishing you had what others have, envious.
jeans
   trousers made from strong, usually blue, cotton.
jeep
   a small, powerful motor car.
jeer
   to make rude remarks about someone.
jelly
   a cold, clear pudding.

jar

jealous

jeep

a b c d e f g h i j k l m n o p q r s t u v w x y z 107

jerk

jerk
  a sudden push or pull.

jersey
  a piece of knitted clothing for the upper part of the body.

jet
  1 a thin stream of water or air.
  2 an engine driven by a stream of air passing through special tubes.

jewel
  a valuable stone often used for ornament.

jewellery
  ornaments that you wear made of precious stones or metal or imitations of these.

jewellery

jigsaw (puzzle)
  a kind of puzzle picture made of little pieces that fit together.

jingle
  to make a ringing sound with small metal objects.

job
  1 the work you do for a living.
  2 a piece of work.

jockey
  the rider of a racehorse.

jog
  1 to run at a slow, steady pace.
  2 to push lightly.

jigsaw

join
  1 to fasten together.
  2 to become a member of a group.

joiner
  a person who works with wood, a carpenter.

joint
  1 the place where two parts fit together.
  2 a large piece of meat.

joke
  something you say to make people laugh.

jolly
  merry, happy, lively.

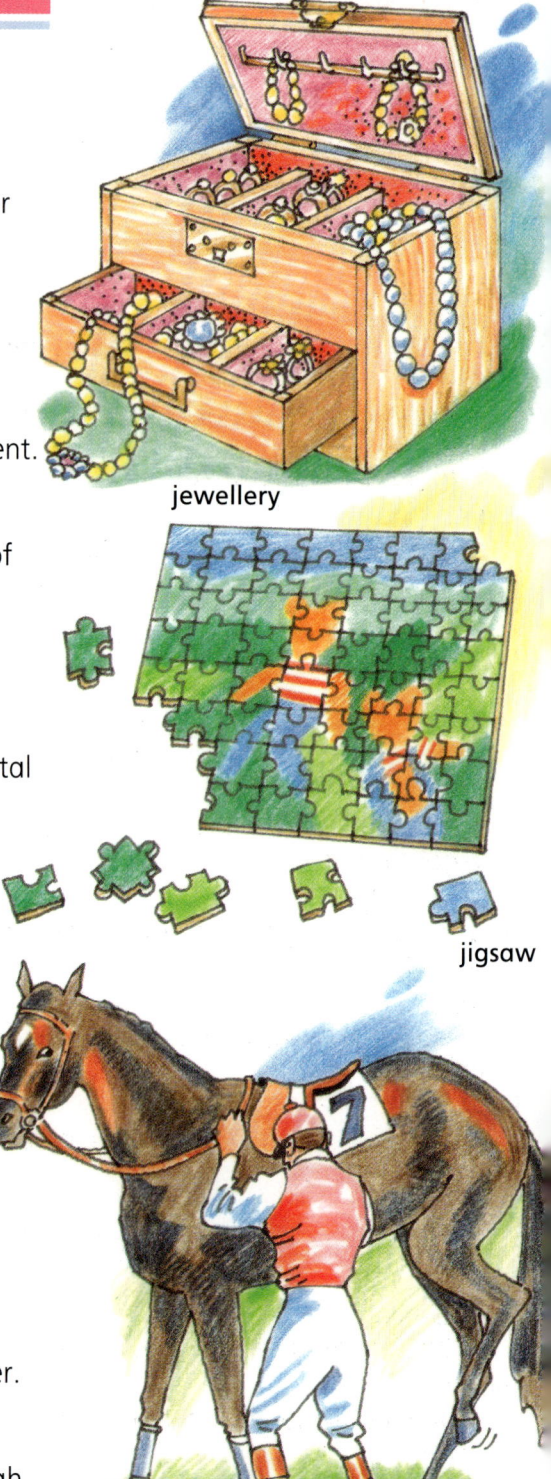

jockey

108 A B C D E F G H I **J** K L M N O P Q R S T U V W X Y Z

jolt

jolt
a sudden jerk.

journey
a trip from place to place.

joy
happiness, gladness.

judge
1 the person in court who has the final say in matters of law.
2 someone who decides the result of a competition.
3 to decide the value of something.

judo
a sport based on a kind of Japanese fighting.

jug
a container for pouring liquids.

juggler
a person who can keep several objects in the air at a time without dropping them.

juice
the liquid which comes from fruit and vegetables.

jumble
a muddle; many things mixed together in an untidy way.

jump
to spring into the air with both feet off the ground.

jumper
a knitted piece of clothing worn on the top part of the body.

junction
a place where two or more railway lines or roads meet.

jungle
a thick forest in very hot countries.

junior
younger or lower in importance than others.

junk
1 rubbish that is of no use to anyone.
2 a Chinese sailing-boat.

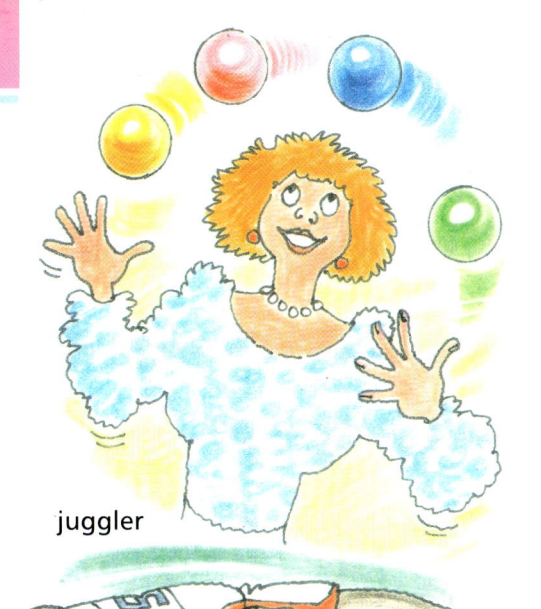

juggler

jump

junction

a b c d e f g h i j k l m n o p q r s t u v w x y z

K k

kangaroo
an Australian animal with long back legs on which it jumps.

karate
a kind of Japanese fighting, now often played as a sport.

keen
1 anxious to do things well, eager.
2 sharp.

keep
to hold; to have for oneself.

kennel
a small house for a dog.

kerb
the edge of a pavement.

kettle
a container with a handle and spout, used to boil water.

key
1 a tool to open or close a lock.
2 a part that you press down on a musical instrument or a typewriter, for example.

kick
to hit with the foot.

kid
1 a young goat, for example.
2 the leather made from a goat's skin.
3 a child.
4 to fool someone.

kidnap
to seize a person and keep them until money is paid for their safe return.

kill
to put to death, to cause to die.

kilogram
a measure of mass equal to 1000 grams.

kangaroo

kettle

kick

ABCDEFGHIJKLMNOPQRSTUVWXYZ

kilometre

kilometre
a measure of length equal to 1000 metres.

kilt
a pleated skirt, usually of tartan cloth, sometimes worn by men in Scotland.

kind
1 a type, a sort.
2 good, helpful, gentle.

king
a male head of a country.

kingdom
an area ruled over by a king or queen.

kipper
a herring split open and smoked.

kiss
to touch with the lips.

kit
things you need in order to do something.

kitchen
a room used for cooking.

kite
a toy for flying at the end of a long string.

kitten
a young cat.

knee
the joint in the middle of the leg.

kneel
to place one or both knees on the ground.

knickers
underpants worn by women and girls.

knife
a sharp blade with a handle used for cutting.

knight
1 a title given to a man by a king or queen; then 'Sir' is put in front of his name.
2 (long ago) a man who fought battles on horseback.

knit
to join loops (of wool, for example) using long needles or machines.

kilt

kiss

kites

a b c d e f g h i j **k** l m n o p q r s t u v w x y z

knob

knob
a round handle used on doors and furniture.

knock
1 to make a tapping noise (at a door, for example).
2 to strike hard.

knot
a fastening made by twisting string or rope.

know
1 to have something in your mind.
2 to recognise someone.

knowledge
something you know and understand.

knuckle
a joint of a finger.

Koran
the religious book of Islam.

knob

knock

clove hitch

slip knot

reef knot

carrick bend

knots

Ll

label
    a paper or card on which information can be written.

labour
    hard work.

lace
    1 an open-work pattern made from fine thread.
    2 a strong string to tie a shoe.

lack
    to be without something.

lad
    a boy.

ladder
    a set of steps for getting up to high places.

ladle
    a large, deep spoon with a long handle (used for serving soup, for example).

lady
    1 a woman.
    2 a title given to a woman, sometimes because of her husband's or father's title.

ladybird
    a small kind of beetle, often red with black spots.

lake
    a large stretch of water with land all round it.

lamb
    a young sheep.

lame
    not able to walk properly, limping.

lamp
    something made for giving light.

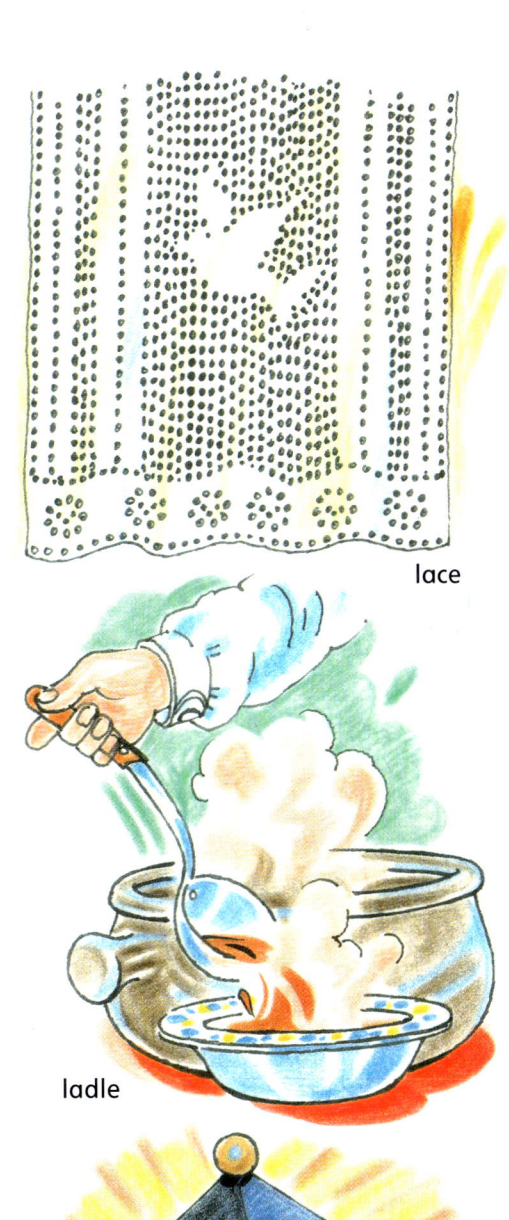

lace

ladle

lamp

land

land
 1 the part of the earth not covered by the sea.
 2 to come to land from air or water.
 3 a country.

lane
 a narrow road.

language
 the words used by the people of a particular country.

lantern
 a case in which a light is carried.

lap
 1 the top of your thighs when you are sitting down.
 2 to drink using the tongue, like a dog or cat.
 3 once round a racetrack.

larch
 a kind of tree with cones which loses its leaves in winter.

large
 big, huge.

lark
 a kind of small songbird.

lash
 1 to fasten tightly with rope or string.
 2 to whip, to hit hard.
 3 a small hair on the eyelid.

lasso (say 'lassoo')
 a rope with a noose at the end for catching animals.

last
 1 coming after all the others.
 2 to go on for a period of time.

late
 1 coming after the right time.
 2 near the end of a period of time.

laugh
 the sound you make when you are amused or happy.

lane

lasso

laugh

laundry

laundry
1 a place where clothing is taken to be washed.
2 a pile of clothing ready for washing or ironing.

lavatory
a toilet.

law
a rule made by the government that everyone must obey.

lawn
an area of short grass in a garden.

lawyer
a person who has studied the law and can advise people about it.

lay
1 to put down.
2 to produce eggs.

lazy
not fond of working, liking to do nothing.

lead (say 'led')
a heavy metal.

lead (say 'leed')
1 to go in front for others to follow.
2 a strap or chain fixed to a dog's collar in order to control the animal.

leader
the person in charge of a group, the head person.

leaf
1 one of the flat, green parts of a tree or other plant.
2 a page of a book.

league
a group of sporting teams who play games against each other to find a winner.

leak
a hole or gap from which liquid or gas can escape.

lay

lead

leak

a b c d e f g h i j k l m n o p q r s t u v w x y z   115

lean

lean
1 to bend towards something.
2 thin, not fat.
3 **lean against** to put your weight against something.

leap
to jump, to spring.

learn
to get to know; to become good at doing something.

leather
an animal's skin which has been prepared for making into shoes or handbags, for example.

leave
1 to go away from.
2 to let something stay where it is.

ledge
a narrow shelf.

leek
a long, white and green vegetable which tastes rather like an onion.

left
the same side of the body as the heart, the opposite of right.

leg
1 one of the limbs with which you walk.
2 one of the supports at the corner of a chair or table, for example.

legal
to do with the law.

legend
a story from long ago, which may not be true.

lemon
a kind of yellow fruit with a sharp taste.

lemonade
a sweet, fizzy drink.

lend
to allow somebody to use something for a time.

length
the distance from one end to the other.

lean against

leeks

length

ABCDEFGHIJK**L**MNOPQRSTUVWXYZ

leopard

leopard
 a large wild animal of the cat family with spotted fur.

leotard
 a close-fitting, single garment worn for sport or exercise (gymnastics, for example).

lesson
 something to be learned.

let
 1 to allow, to permit.
 2 to allow someone to use a building in return for a rent.

letter
 1 a written message sent to somebody.
 2 one of the signs we use for writing, such as a, b, c.

lettuce
 a kind of broad-leaved, green vegetable used in salads.

level
 1 the same height all along, flat.
 2 equal.

lever
 a strong metal bar for lifting or moving things.

liar
 a person who tells lies.

librarian
 a person who works in a library.

library
 a room or building where books are kept.

licence
 a printed paper that gives you permission to do something.

lick
 to wet or rub with the tongue.

lid
 a cover that can be opened or taken off.

lie
 1 to rest in a flat position.
 2 to say things that are not true.
 3 something which is not true.

leopard

leotard

library

a b c d e f g h i j k **l** m n o p q r s t u v w x y z   117

life

life
the time when you are alive.

lifeboat
a boat kept ready to go to the help of people in danger on the sea.

lift
1 to raise.
2 a machine which carries people or goods up and down in a building.
3 a ride in someone's vehicle.

light
1 brightness, the opposite of darkness.
2 pale in colour, not dark.
3 having little weight, easy to lift.
4 to make something burn (for example, a fire or a lamp).

lighthouse
a tower with a bright light on top to warn ships of danger.

lightning
a flash of light you see in the sky during a thunderstorm.

like
1 to be fond of.
2 the same as, similar to.

likely
what you would expect.

lilac
1 a kind of small tree with sweet-smelling purple or white flowers.
2 a pale-purple colour, like these flowers.

lily
a beautiful flower, often white in colour.

limb
an arm, a leg or a wing.

lime
1 a green fruit like a small lemon.
2 a kind of tree with large, pale-green leaves.
3 a white powder made from limestone.

limestone
a greyish-white rock.

lifeboat

lighthouse

lime

limit

limit
  the end, as far as you can go.

limp
  1 to walk as if one foot or leg has been hurt.
  2 not firm or stiff.

line
  1 a long, thin mark.
  2 a piece of rope or string.
  3 people or things standing one behind the other.

linen
  a kind of thin cloth (used for making sheets or tablecloths, for example).

liner
  a large passenger ship.

lion
  a large wild animal of the cat family, found in Africa and India.

lip
  one of the soft, round edges of the mouth.

lipstick
  colouring for the lips.

liquid
  something which flows (for example, water or milk).

liquorice
  a kind of chewy, black sweet made from a plant root.

list
  a number of names or things written down one after the other.

listen
  1 to try to hear.
  2 to take notice of what someone is saying.

litre
  a measure of liquid.

litter
  1 rubbish lying about.
  2 a number of animals born together.

little
  small, tiny, not big.

liner

lipstick

litter

live

live
1 to stay in a place.
2 to be alive.

lively
full of life, active.

lizard
an animal with four short legs, a long tail and skin like a snake.

load
1 as much as can be carried at one time.
2 to put goods onto a ship or vehicle.
3 to put bullets into a gun.

loaf
a large piece of bread which you cut in slices.

loan
something that is lent or borrowed.

lobster
a kind of large shellfish with claws.

local
near a particular place, near where you are.

lock
1 to fasten something so that only a key will open it.
2 a place in a canal where ships are raised or lowered.
3 a piece of hair.

locust
an insect like a grasshopper which destroys crops.

loft
the space under the roof of a building.

log
1 a part of a tree sawn off for building or for firewood.
2 a ship's diary.

lollipop
a sweet on the end of a stick.

lonely
1 feeling sad and alone; without friends.
2 (of a house, for example) with no others near it.

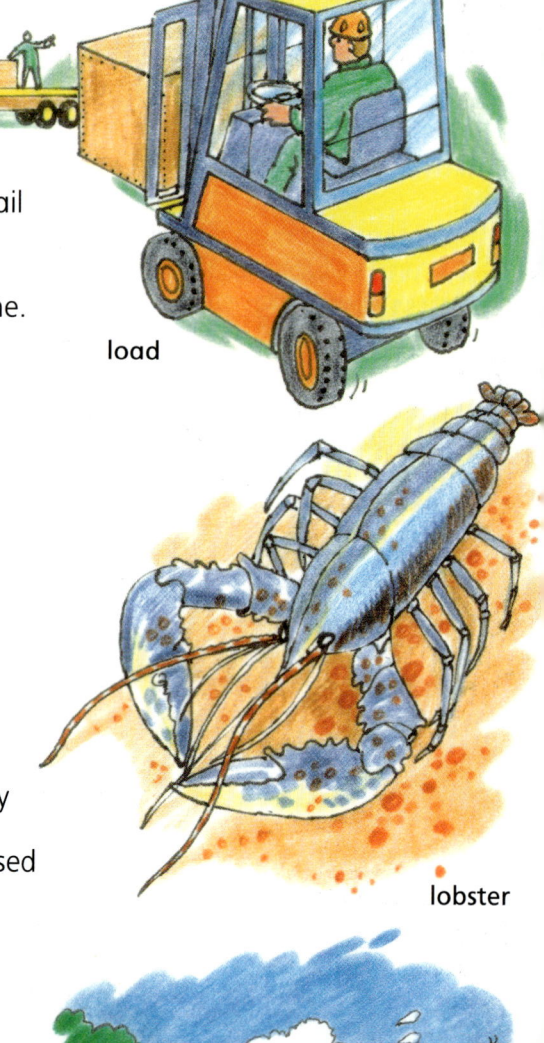

load

lobster

lock

long

long
1 of great length, not short.
2 to wish for something very much.

look
1 to try to see.
2 to appear to be, to seem.

loop
a shape like a ring made in string or rope, for example.

loose
not tied or fixed, free to move, slack.

lord
a title given to a man by a king or queen.

lorry
a large motor vehicle for carrying heavy loads.

lose
1 not to be able to find something, to stop having.
2 to be beaten, not to win.

loss
something you have lost.

loud
making a lot of noise, easily heard.

lounge
1 a sitting room.
2 to act lazily.

love
to like very much.

lovely
beautiful.

low
1 not high, near to the ground or the bottom of something.
2 quiet, not loud.
3 (of a sound) deep, low-pitched.

loyal
able to be trusted to defend friends or country.

luck
fortune, chance.

lucky
having good luck.

long

lorry

loud

luggage

luggage
bags and suitcases you take with you when travelling.

lullaby
a quiet song to send a baby to sleep.

lump
1 a swelling.
2 a piece of something.

lunch
a meal eaten in the middle of the day.

lung
one of the two parts of the body with which you breathe.

luxury
something expensive you like having but do not need.

luggage

lullaby

- Left lung
- Right lung
- Heart
- Ribs
- Stomach

lungs

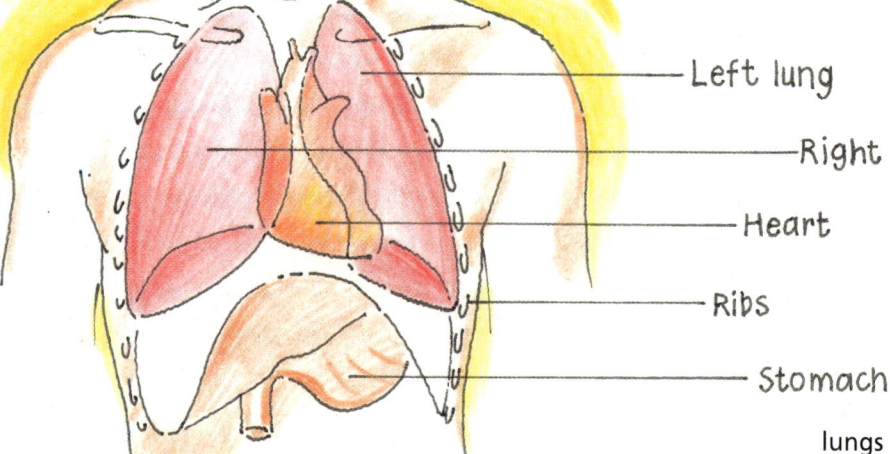

M m

machine
  something made out of many parts that work together to do a job.

mackerel
  a kind of sea-fish used as food.

mackintosh
  a raincoat, a waterproof coat.

mad
  1 crazy; very foolish.
  2 very angry.

magazine
  a paper containing stories and pictures, sold every week or month.

maggot
  a grub which turns into a fly (sometimes found on bad meat, for example).

magic
  1 strange and wonderful things which happen.
  2 clever or strange tricks done to amuse.

magnet
  a piece of iron or steel which attracts other pieces of iron or steel.

magnificent
  splendid.

magpie
  a black and white bird with a long tail which likes to pick up brightly-coloured objects.

maid
  1 a woman servant.
  2 an old-fashioned word for a girl.

mail
  1 letters and parcels sent by post.
  2 a kind of armour worn by soldiers long ago.

main
  most important, chief.

machine

magazine

magic

a b c d e f g h i j k l m n o p q r s t u v w x y z

major

major
1 an officer in the army.
2 the chief, the most important.

make
1 to build; to create.
2 to force somebody to do something.

male
a person or animal that can become a father; a man or boy.

mammal
an animal which feeds its young with its own milk.

mammoth
1 a kind of large elephant of long ago.
2 very big, huge.

man
a grown-up male person.

manage
1 to be able to do something.
2 to take charge of something.

mane
the long hair on the neck of an animal (for example, like a horse or lion).

manner
1 the way in which we behave.
2 the way in which a thing is done.

manners
behaviour, especially good behaviour towards other people.

mansion
a very large house.

manufacture
to make things in a factory by using machinery.

map
a drawing of a place or country as it looks from the air.

marble
1 a hard stone which can be smoothly polished.
2 a small, round glass or stone ball used as a toy.

major

mammal

mansion

march

march
1 to walk in step with others.
2 a piece of music to which people march, especially soldiers.

mare
a female horse.

margarine
a food made from vegetable oils which is often used instead of butter.

mark
1 a sign put on something.
2 a spot, a stain.
3 the number you reach in a test.
4 to put a mark on.

market
a place, often in the open air, where goods are bought and sold.

marmalade
a kind of jam made with oranges or lemons, for example.

maroon
1 a very dark red colour.
2 to leave someone somewhere where they cannot get away (for example, on an island).

marriage
a wedding.

marry
to become someone's husband or wife.

marsh
wet land, a swamp, a bog.

marvellous
wonderful.

mascot
a charm, a thing or animal supposed to bring good luck.

masculine
concerning men and boys.

mash
to crush to a soft, smooth state.

mask
a covering for the face.

market

marmalade

mascot

a b c d e f g h i j k l **m** n o p q r s t u v w x y z   125

mass

mass
1 a large amount of something.
2 a crowd of people.
3 a religious ceremony, especially in a Roman Catholic church.
4 how heavy something is.

massive
very large, enormous.

mast
the tall pole used to hold up the sails on a ship.

master
the chief man, the man in charge.

mat
1 a small rug.
2 a small piece of material for putting under plates and dishes.

match
1 a small, thin stick with a tip which catches fire when rubbed.
2 a game between two teams.
3 to be the same as something else.

mate
a companion.

material
1 anything from which things can be made.
2 cloth.

mathematics
the study of numbers, shapes and measurements.

matter
1 to be important.
2 something you think about.

mattress
a large, thick layer of material on which you sleep.

mayor
the chief person in a town.

maze
a lot of paths and lines arranged so that it is difficult to find your way through them.

meadow
a field of grass.

mast

maze

meadow

ABCDEFGHIJKL**M**NOPQRSTUVWXYZ

meal

meal
1 the food you eat at a certain time of day.
2 grain ground into a kind of flour.

mean
1 not generous.
2 to have a meaning.
3 **mean to** to have it in your mind to.

meaning
what you have in your mind when you say or write something, an explanation.

measles
an illness which gives you red spots.

measure
to find out how long or heavy something is.

meat
flesh from an animal used as food.

mechanic
a person who makes or repairs machinery.

medal
a disc of metal given as a reward for something you have done.

meddle
to interfere with things which are not your business.

medicine
something you take to make you better when you are ill.

medium
not big or small, in between.

meet
1 to come together.
2 to go to see and greet someone.

melody
a tune.

melon
a kind of large, juicy fruit with a green or yellow skin.

melt
to become liquid because of heat.

member
a person who belongs to a group.

mechanic

medal

melon

a b c d e f g h i j k l m n o p q r s t u v w x y z

memory

memory
  1 the part of the brain with which you remember.
  2 a thought about the past.

mend
  to put right, to repair.

mental
  to do with the mind.

menu
  a list of things you can eat in a restaurant.

merchant
  a person who buys and sells.

merry
  happy, cheerful, joyful.

mess
  things mixed together in an untidy way.

message
  news sent from one person to another.

metal
  materials such as iron, steel, gold, silver and brass.

meteor
  a small object from space which travels very fast and burns out when it enters the earth's atmosphere.

meter
  a machine for measuring such things as gas or electricity.

metre
  a measure of length equal to 100 centimetres.

microphone
  an instrument which picks up sounds and makes them louder.

microscope
  an instrument used to make very small things look much bigger.

midday
  twelve o'clock in the day.

middle
  the part of something that is the same distance from each end or side.

mess

meter

microphone

midnight

midnight
　twelve o'clock at night.
mild
　1 gentle, not rough.
　2 not too hot or cold.
mile
　a measure of length.
milk
　a white liquid produced by mothers and some female animals to feed their babies.
mill
　1 a place where grain is ground into flour or meal.
　2 a kind of factory, especially one where cloth is made.
mime
　to use actions instead of words to show the meaning of something.
mimic
　to speak or act like someone else.
mind
　1 a person's way of thinking.
　2 to look after.
　3 to object to something.
mine
　1 belonging to me.
　2 a place where coal and other minerals are dug from the earth.
mineral
　things such as rock which are dug out of the earth.
mingle
　to mix.
miniature
　very small, but like something bigger.
minister
　1 a person in charge of a church, a clergyman.
　2 an important member of a government.
mint
　1 a plant used to flavour food.
　2 a sweet flavoured with mint.
　3 a place where coins are made.

mill

mine

miniature

a b c d e f g h i j k l **m** n o p q r s t u v w x y z　129

minus

minus
  less than, without; the sign −.

minute (say '<u>min</u>it')
  a length of time equal to 60 seconds.

minute (say 'my<u>newt</u>')
  very small.

miracle
  a strange and wonderful happening which is thought to be the work of God.

mirror
  a piece of glass in which you can see yourself.

mischief
  silly things done to harm or annoy others.

miser
  a person who has plenty of money but tries not to spend any.

miserable
  full of sadness.

misery
  great unhappiness, sorrow.

miss
  1 not to see or find; not to succeed.
  2 **Miss** a title given to an unmarried woman or girl.

missionary
  a person who is sent to other places to teach people about religion.

mist
  drops of water in the air which stop you from seeing properly, fog.

mistake
  something you have done or thought which is wrong, an error.

mistletoe
  an evergreen plant with white berries, often used as a Christmas decoration.

mistress
  the chief woman, the woman in charge.

mitten
  a glove with only two parts, one for the fingers and one for the thumb.

mirror

miss

mistletoe

mix

mix
to put things together by stirring or shaking, for example.

mixture
things mixed together.

moan
a low sound made when you are in pain or unhappy.

moat
a ditch round a castle to keep it safe from attack.

mock
to make fun of someone, especially by doing the same as they do.

model
1 a copy of something.
2 a pattern to be followed.
3 a person whose job is to wear clothes in order to display them (for example, for a photograph.

modern
up-to-date, belonging to the present time.

moist
a little wet, damp.

mole
1 a small, furry animal which burrows underground.
2 a small, dark spot on the skin.

moment
a very short space of time.

monastery
a place where monks live.

money
the coins and pieces of paper you use for buying and selling.

mongrel
a dog of two or more breeds.

monk
a man who has given his life to his religion and who lives in a monastery.

monkey
an animal with a long tail and with hands and feet.

mix

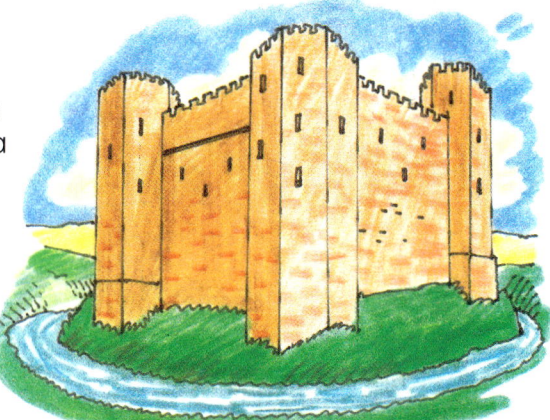

moat

mole

a b c d e f g h i j k l m n o p q r s t u v w x y z

monster

monster
   a large, frightening animal, especially an imaginary one.

month
   1 one of the twelve parts of the year (for example, August).
   2 a period of four weeks.

mood
   the way you feel.

moon
   the planet that goes round the earth and is sometimes seen shining in the sky.

moon

moor
   1 a large area of rough ground, covered with grass and heather.
   2 to fasten a boat with a rope.

mop
   soft material at the end of a long pole, used for cleaning.

more
   a greater number.

morning
   the part of the day before noon.

mosque
   a place where Muslims worship.

moss
   a furry, green plant which grows on wet stones and trees.

mop

most
   the greatest number or amount.

moth
   an insect like a butterfly which usually flies at night.

mother
   a female parent.

motor
   an engine to make things move or turn.

motorway
   a road specially made to take fast traffic.

mould
   1 to make something into a new shape.
   2 a container for shaping things.

mould

mound

mound
    a large heap; a small hill.

mount
    to get onto (a horse or a bicycle, for example).

mountain
    a very high hill.

mourn
    to be very sad for the death of someone or for the loss of something.

mouse
    a very small animal with a long tail.

moustache
    hair growing on the upper lip.

mouth
    1 the part of the head with which you speak, eat and drink.
    2 where a river goes into the sea.

move
    to go or take from one place to another.

Mr (say 'mister')
    a title given to a man.

Mrs (say 'missiz')
    a title given to a married woman.

Ms
    a title given to a woman who may or may not be married.

mud
    wet earth.

muddle
    a mixed-up state.

mug
    a big cup with straight sides.

multiply
    to increase something a number of times.

mumble
    to speak in a way that is difficult to hear and understand.

mummy
    1 a dead body that has been preserved.
    2 **Mummy** or **Mum** a name for your mother.

mount

moustache

move

a b c d e f g h i j k l **m** n o p q r s t u v w x y z

mumps

mumps
a painful illness of the neck.

munch
to eat noisily.

murder
to kill someone on purpose.

murmur
to speak very quietly.

muscle
one of the parts of the body that help you to move.

muscle

museum
a building where old and interesting things can be seen.

mushroom
a plant which can be eaten and is shaped like a small umbrella.

music
pleasant sounds made by voices singing or by instruments.

musical
1 to do with music.
2 a special type of film or a play using music.

musician
a person who plays a musical instrument.

mussel
a kind of shellfish used as food.

mustard
a hot-tasting yellow powder or paste used to flavour food.

mushrooms

mutter
to speak or complain in a low voice.

mysterious
very strange.

mystery
something strange which cannot be explained.

mussels

A B C D E F G H I J K L **M** N O P Q R S T U V W X Y Z

Nn

nag
  to keep finding fault with someone.

nail
  1 a small, pointed piece of metal used to join pieces of wood together.
  2 the hard, shining covering on the end of a finger or toe.

naked
  not wearing any clothes, not covered, bare.

name
  what you call someone or something, the word you use when talking about a person or thing.

napkin
  a small piece of cloth or paper used at the table to keep your clothes clean.

nappy
  a piece of towel or padded paper wrapped round a baby's bottom.

narrow
  not far across, not wide.

nasty
  not pleasant; not good to taste; not kind.

nation
  the people of one country.

native
  a person born in a certain place.

natural
  made by nature, not made by people.

nature
  1 everything in the world not made by people; all animals, plants and rocks.
  2 the way people or other living things behave.

naughty
  badly behaved.

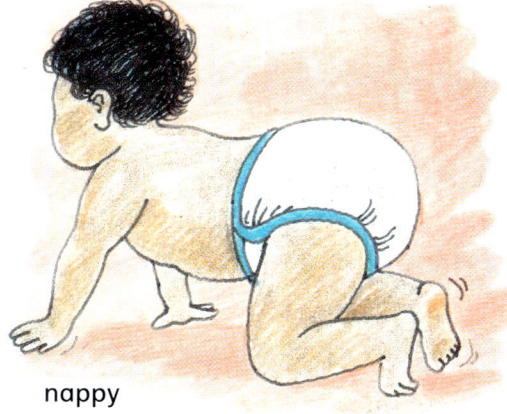

napkin

nappy

narrow

navigate

navigate
　to tell which way a ship, aeroplane or car should go.

navy
　1 a country's warships and sailors.
　2 a dark-blue colour.

near
　close to; not far away.

nearly
　almost, not quite.

neat
　tidy and clean.

neck
　the part of the body joining the head and shoulders.

necklace
　a string of beads or jewels worn round the neck.

need
　1 to want badly.
　2 **need to** to have to.

needle
　a thin, sharp piece of metal with a hole at one end, used for sewing.

neglect
　not to do something that should be done; not to look after.

neigh
　the sound a horse makes.

neighbour
　a person who lives next door or quite near.

nephew
　a son of a brother or sister.

nerve
　one of the small parts of the body which carry messages to and from the brain.

nervous
　afraid; easily frightened or worried.

nest
　a place used as a home by birds and some animals.

neat

neighbour

nest

net

net
something made of string or wire which can catch solid objects.

netball
a team game in which a ball is thrown into a high net.

nettle
a wild plant which can sting when touched.

new
just made or bought; not used or known before.

news
telling or writing about something that has happened.

newspaper
folded sheets of paper printed every day or every week giving news.

next
1 nearest, with nothing in between.
2 following.

nibble
to eat in tiny bites.

nice
pleasant.

nickname
a name that is not your real name.

niece
a daughter of a brother or sister.

night
the time of darkness.

nightmare
a bad or frightening dream.

nimble
quick and light on your feet.

nip
to bite, to pinch.

nod
to bend your head forward quickly, often as a sign that you mean 'yes'.

noise
a sound, often loud and unpleasant.

nettle

nibble

night

a b c d e f g h i j k l m **n** o p q r s t u v w x y z   137

nonsense

nonsense
  words that have no sense or meaning, foolishness.

noon
  twelve o'clock midday.

noose
  a loop in a rope which can be made tighter by pulling.

normal
  usual, the same as others.

north
  the direction that is on the left as you face the rising sun.

nose
  the part of your face with which you breathe and smell things.

nostril
  one of the two openings in your nose.

note
  1 a short letter.
  2 a single sound in music.
  3 a piece of paper money.

notice
  1 to see something.
  2 a piece of paper, often pinned to a wall, which tells you something.

now
  at this moment, at this time.

nudge
  a slight push.

nuisance
  something which annoys you or holds you up.

numb
  not having any feeling.

number
  1 a word or figure, such as one, two, three, 1, 2, 3, which tells you how many.
  2 more than one person or thing.

nun
  a woman who has given her life to her religion and lives in a convent.

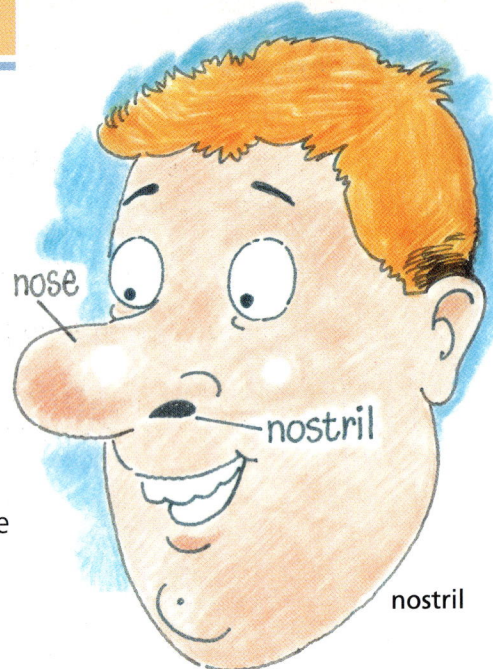

nostril

notice

nuisance

nurse

nurse
    a person trained to look after sick people or young children.

nursery
    1 a room or building for very young children.
    2 a place where young plants are grown.

nut
    1 a seed with a hard shell, used for food.
    2 a piece of metal which screws onto a bolt.

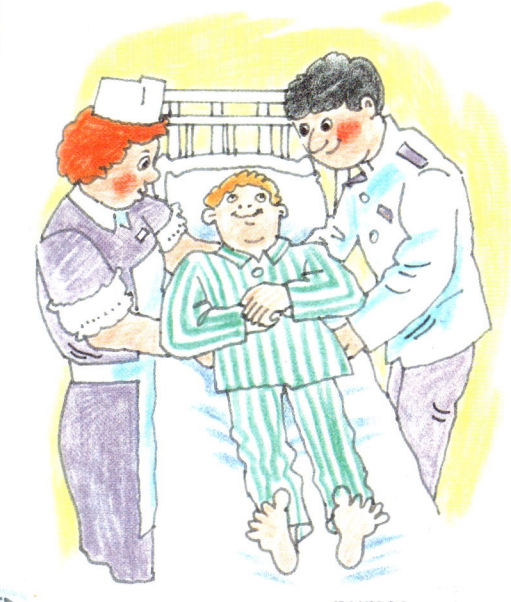

nurses

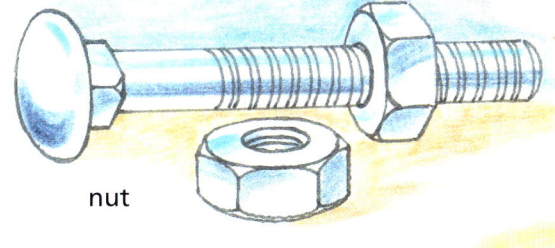

nut

nursery

a b c d e f g h i j k l m **n** o p q r s t u v w x y z

O o

oak
a kind of large tree with hard wood.

oar
a long piece of wood, flat at one end, used to push a boat through the water.

oasis
a place in the desert where water can be found and some plants grow.

oats
a plant which produces grain used for food (porridge, for example).

object
something that you can see or touch.

object
to say that you do not like or agree to something.

oblong
a shape which is longer than it is broad, like this page.

observe
to see, to look at, to notice.

ocean
a very large sea.

o'clock
the hour shown by the clock.

octopus
a kind of sea creature with eight arms called tentacles.

odd
1 not even: 1, 3, 5 are **odd** numbers.
2 strange, unusual.

offend
to hurt someone's feelings.

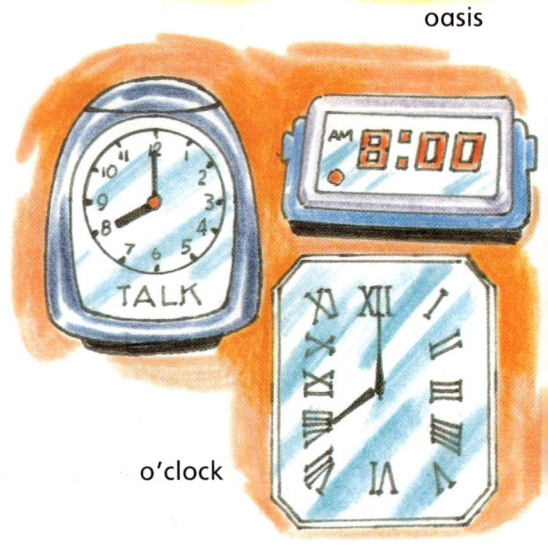

oars

oasis

o'clock

offer

offer
1 to say that you are ready to do something.
2 to hold something out for someone to take.

office
a place where people do business.

officer
1 a person who is in charge of other people (for example, in the army).
2 a person with an important position in an organisation.

often
many times.

ogre
(in stories) a giant who eats people.

oil
a greasy liquid.

ointment
a healing cream put on cuts and bruises.

old
1 of great age, not new or young.
2 having lived for a certain number of years.

omelette
eggs beaten together and fried.

once
1 one time.
2 in the past.

onion
a kind of vegetable with a strong smell, made up of a lot of layers.

only
1 by itself, singly.
2 not more than.

ooze
to flow slowly.

open
not shut, not covered over.

operate
1 to work a machine.
2 to cut the body open to do something to make it healthy again.

office

oil

open

a b c d e f g h i j k l m n o p q r s t u v w x y z 141

opinion

opinion
what you think about something.

opposite
1 the side facing you.
2 as different as possible.
3 on the other side of a place or an argument.

orange
1 a kind of juicy, reddish-yellow fruit grown in some hot countries.
2 the colour of this fruit.

orchard
a place where fruit trees are grown.

orchestra
a large group of musicians playing together.

order
1 neatly arranged things or ideas.
2 to say what must be done.

ordinary
usual, what you expect.

organ
1 a large musical instrument with many pipes, played like a piano.
2 a part of the inside of the body.

organisation
1 a system; a plan of work.
2 a society; a business.

original
the earliest, the first one.

ornament
something used for decoration, especially in a room.

orphan
a child whose father and mother have both died.

ostrich
a very large African bird which cannot fly.

other
not the same, different.

otter
a kind of fish-eating animal which lives near water.

orchard

ornament

ostrich

ABCDEFGHIJKLMN**O**PQRSTUVWXYZ

ounce

ounce
a measure of weight.

out
1 not inside.
2 not lit.

outfit
a complete set of clothes or equipment.

outlaw
(long ago) a person who continually broke the law.

oval
egg-shaped.

oven
a heated box for cooking and baking.

over
1 above.
2 done; finished.
3 more than.
4 across.

overalls
a special piece of clothing for working in, worn over your ordinary clothes.

overtake
to catch up with and then pass.

owe
to be in debt; to have to pay.

owl
a bird which has large eyes and hunts at night.

own
1 belonging to yourself.
2 to have.

oxygen
a gas without taste, smell or colour which is an important part of air and water and is necessary to keep you alive.

oven

overtake

oxygen

P p

pace
1 a step, a stride.
2 the speed at which you walk, run or move.

pack
1 to put into a box, parcel or suitcase.
2 a group of things such as playing-cards.
3 a group of animals that hunt together.

packet
a small box or container made of plastic, paper or cardboard.

packets

pad
1 several sheets of paper stuck together at the top edge.
2 a piece of soft material such as cotton wool.
3 the thick skin on the feet of some animals.

paddle
1 a piece of wood with a broad, flat end for driving a canoe or small boat.
2 to walk in shallow water.

padlock
a small lock on a ring which can be fixed to the thing it is locking.

page
a leaf of a book or newspaper.

pail
a bucket.

pain
the feeling of being hurt, suffering.

paint
a coloured liquid used to colour something.

painting
a picture which is painted.

pair
two things of the same kind, a set of two.

paddle

padlock

144 A B C D E F G H I J K L M N O P Q R S T U V W X Y Z

palace

palace
 a large building often lived in by kings and queens.

pale
 with little colour.

palm
 1 a tree which grows in hot countries.
 2 the flat front of the hand.

pan
 a round metal pot with a long handle, used for cooking.

pancake
 a thin cake of flour, eggs and milk which is fried in a pan.

panda
 a black and white animal like a small bear, found in China.

pane
 a piece of glass for a window.

panic
 sudden alarm or fear which makes someone do things without thinking.

pant
 to breathe quickly as though you are short of breath.

panther
 a large, black wild animal of the cat family.

pantomime
 a nursery story performed on the stage with music and songs.

pants
 underpants.

paper
 1 material for writing on, making books and wrapping things, for example.
 2 a newspaper.

parable
 a story, usually from the Bible, which has a special meaning.

parachute
 cloth shaped like an umbrella, used when jumping from an aircraft.

palms

pancake

panda

a b c d e f g h i j k l m n o p q r s t u v w x y z   145

parade

parade
1 a marching display by people in uniform.
2 to march up and down.

paradise
a place of complete happiness, heaven.

paraffin
a thin oil used in lamps and stoves.

paralysed
unable to move some or all of the body (because of serious injury, for example).

parcel
something wrapped up for posting or carrying.

parent
a father or mother.

park
1 a piece of land, usually with grass and flowers, where you can go to play or enjoy yourself.
2 a games field.
3 to leave a vehicle somewhere for a time.

parliament
1 a group of people who make the laws of a country.
2 the place where they meet.

parrot
a bird which has bright feathers and a sharp, hooked beak.

parsley
a herb used in cooking.

parsnip
a pale root vegetable.

part
1 a piece of a whole thing.
2 a share in some activity.
3 to split up, to separate.

partner
1 one of two people playing a game or dancing together, for example.
2 a person sharing in a business.

party
a group of people gathered together to enjoy themselves.

parliament

parrot

party

ABCDEFGHIJKLMNOPQRSTUVWXYZ

pass

pass
1 to leave behind, to go past.
2 to get through a test.
3 a gap in the mountains.
4 a piece of paper that lets you go into places.

passage
1 a narrow way through.
2 a piece taken from a book or story.

passenger
a person who travels by train, ship or aeroplane, for example.

passport
a kind of pass which allows you to travel abroad.

past
1 the time that has gone before.
2 up to and away from.

paste
a wet and sticky mixture (toothpaste, for example).

pastry
a mixture of flour, water and fat used for baking pies and tarts.

pat
to touch gently with the hand.

patch
a small piece of material used to repair a hole (in clothes, for example).

path
a narrow track for walking.

patient
1 able to wait calmly for things to be right.
2 someone who is ill and seeing a doctor or dentist, for example.

patrol
a small group of policemen or soldiers, for example, on the lookout for something.

patter
the sound made by raindrops or running feet.

passengers

patch

patient

a b c d e f g h i j k l m n o p q r s t u v w x y z   147

pattern

pattern
1 lines and shapes arranged to look attractive.
2 a plan to follow when making something.

pause
a short stop or wait.

pavement
the part at each side of the street you walk on.

paw
a foot of an animal such as a dog or cat.

pay
1 to hand over money for something.
2 money you are given for working.

pea
a round, green seed which grows in a pod, used as food.

peace
1 quietness, stillness, calm.
2 not being at war.

peach
a kind of soft, juicy fruit with a large, hard seed inside.

peacock
a large male bird with a beautiful tail shaped like a fan. The female is called a **peahen**.

peak
1 the top of a hill or mountain.
2 the front part of a cap which sticks out.

peal
1 the sound of very big bells.
2 the sound of thunder.

peanut
a small, round, hard seed like a nut, used as food.

pear
a large, soft, juicy, yellow or green fruit.

pearl
a precious gem found in some oyster shells, for example.

paw

peas

peak

148 A B C D E F G H I J K L M N O P Q R S T U V W X Y Z

pebble

pebble
　a small, smooth, rounded stone.

peck
　to pick up food with the beak, to poke at.

peculiar
　strange, unusual.

pedal
　a bar or lever which you move with the feet (to drive a machine, for example).

pedestrian
　a person who is walking.

peel
　1 the outside skin of fruit or vegetables.
　2 to take off the outer covering.

peep
　to look at quickly and secretly, to glance.

peer
　1 to look at closely.
　2 a person of high rank.

peg
　1 a small hook for hanging clothes on.
　2 a small clip for fixing clothes to a washing line.

pelican
　a large bird which stores food in a pouch under its beak.

pen
　1 a tool used for writing with ink.
　2 a place fenced in to keep animals together.

penalty
　a punishment for breaking a rule or the law.

pence
　the plural of **penny**.

pencil
　a writing tool made of wood with a grey or coloured centre.

penguin
　a large, black and white sea bird which can swim but cannot fly, found near the South Pole.

peel

pen

penguins

a b c d e f g h i j k l m n o p q r s t u v w x y z   149

penknife

penknife
a small knife with a folding blade.

penny
a small British coin; 100 of these are equal to a pound.

people
men, women and children.

pepper
a hot-tasting powder used for flavouring.

peppermint
a flavouring used in sweets and toothpastes, for example.

perch
1 a bar on which a bird can rest.
2 to sit on the edge of something.
3 a kind of large freshwater fish.

perfect
without fault, complete.

perform
to act, to do.

perfume
scent, a pleasant smell.

perhaps
maybe, possibly.

period
a length of time.

permanent
not coming to an end, for all time.

permission
being allowed to do something.

permit
to allow, to let someone do something.

person
a man, a woman or a child.

persuade
to talk to a person until he or she does as you wish.

pest
a person, an animal or an insect that annoys you or causes damage.

pester
to keep annoying somebody.

perch

perform

perfume

pet

pet
   an animal which you keep for pleasure.

petal
   one of the usually brightly-coloured separate parts of a flower.

petrol
   the liquid that drives the engine of a motor car, for example.

pheasant
   a large, colourful game bird with a long tail.

phone
   1 short for **telephone**.
   2 to use a telephone.

photograph
   a picture taken using a camera.

physical
   belonging to the natural world or the body.

pianist
   a person who plays the piano.

piano
   a large musical instrument played by pressing the keys.

pick
   1 to gather flowers or fruit, for example.
   2 to choose.
   3 a pointed metal tool with a wooden handle for making holes in hard ground.

pickles
   vegetables kept in vinegar.

picnic
   a meal eaten in the open air.

picture
   a drawing, a painting or a photograph of something.

pie
   fruit or meat cooked in a pastry case.

piece
   a part of something larger.

pier
   a landing-stage built out into the water for ships.

pet

pianist

piece

a b c d e f g h i j k l m n o **p** q r s t u v w x y z   151

pierce

pierce
to make a hole in something, to stab.

pig
an animal kept on a farm; pork and bacon are made from it.

pigeon
a greyish bird which makes a soft noise.

piglet
a young pig.

pile
a heap.

pilgrim
a person who travels to visit a holy place.

pill
a small ball of medicine for swallowing.

pillar
an upright post, often used to hold up part of a building.

pillow
a cushion to rest your head on in bed.

pilot
1 a person who controls an aeroplane.
2 a person who goes on board a ship to guide it into harbour.

pimple
a small, usually red or yellow, swelling under the skin.

pin
a thin, sharp piece of metal used for holding things together.

pinch
1 to nip tightly with the fingers.
2 a very small amount (of salt, for example).

pine
1 to long for something or somebody very much.
2 a kind of tall tree on which cones grow.

pineapple
a kind of large, juicy fruit grown in hot countries.

pink
a very light red colour.

pillars

pilot

pineapple

pint

pint
   a measure of liquid.

pip
   a small seed (in an apple or an orange, for example).

pipe
   1 a tube to carry a gas or liquid from one place to another.
   2 a small bowl with a stem for smoking tobacco.
   3 a musical instrument.

pirate
   a sea robber.

pistol
   a short handgun, a revolver.

pit
   1 a hole in the ground.
   2 a coalmine.

pitch
   1 a stretch of ground for playing games.
   2 to put up a tent.
   3 to throw.

pity
   1 feeling sorry for somebody.
   2 something you are sorry about.

pizza
   a flat, open pie topped with cheese, tomatoes and other types of food.

place
   1 a position on the earth's surface.
   2 a space for something.

plain
   1 ordinary, simple.
   2 easily seen or heard.
   3 a flat piece of land.

plait (say 'plat')
   to twist together, one over another, three or more strands of hair or rope.

plan
   1 a drawing to help you to make something.
   2 to arrange.

pint

pitch

plait

a b c d e f g h i j k l m n o p q r s t u v w x y z

plane

plane
1 short for **aeroplane**.
2 a tool for smoothing wood.

planet
one of the large objects, such as the earth, that go round the sun.

plank
a long, flat piece of wood.

plant
1 something which grows from roots in the ground.
2 to put seeds into soil so that they will grow.

plaster
1 a paste to cover walls which goes grey and hard when dried.
2 a covering you put on a cut to protect it.

plastic
a light and strong man-made material used to make many different objects.

plate
a flat dish from which you eat food.

platform
1 a raised place, usually in a hall.
2 the place in a station where you get on and off trains.

play
1 a story which is acted.
2 to enjoy yourself, especially in a game.
3 to make sounds on a musical instrument.

pleasant
delightful, pleasing.

please
1 to make somebody happy.
2 a polite word used when asking for something.

pleasure
happiness, joy.

pleat
a fold which is pressed into clothes.

plenty
more than enough.

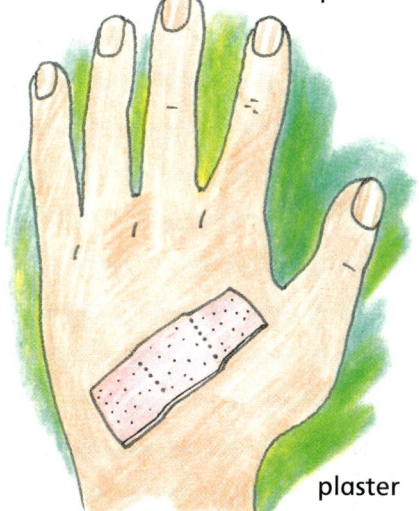

plant

plaster

play

pliers

pliers
a tool with handles and a head for gripping and cutting things.

plot
1 the story of a play.
2 a piece of ground.
3 a secret plan.

plough
a machine for breaking up the soil.

pluck
1 to take the feathers from a dead bird.
2 to gather flowers or fruit.
3 to pull and then let go (the strings of a guitar, for example).

plug
1 a stopper for a bath or a bowl.
2 something you put into a socket to get electricity.

plum
a soft, red or purple fruit with a large, hard seed in it.

plumber
a person who fits and repairs water and gas pipes.

plump
pleasantly fat.

plunge
to dive in.

plural
numbering more than one.

plus
added to; the sign +.

poach
1 to cook gently in water (for example, an egg).
2 to hunt animals or catch fish without permission.

pocket
a bag sewn into your clothes to hold money and other things.

pod
a long case on a plant with seeds in it.

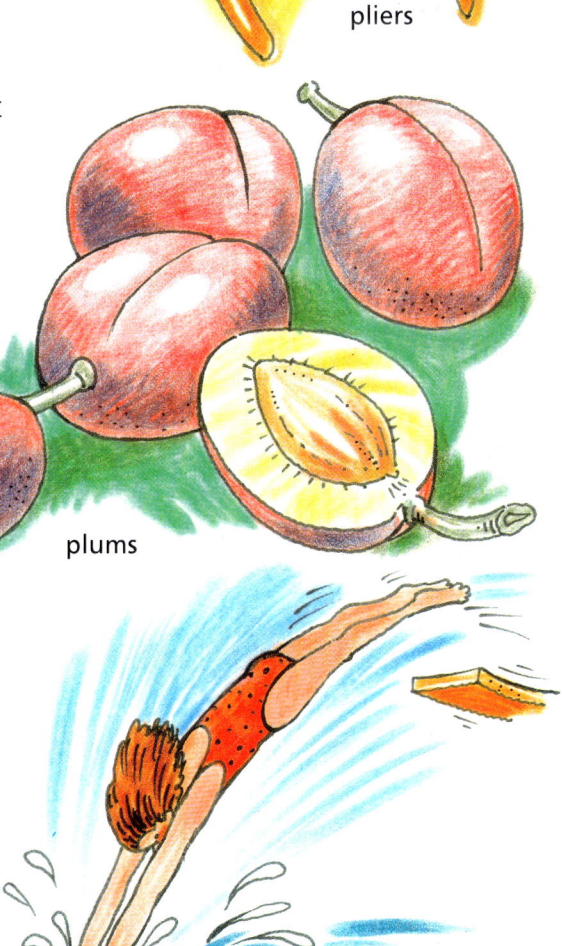

pliers

plums

plunge

a b c d e f g h i j k l m n o p q r s t u v w x y z 155

poem

poem
  a piece of poetry.

poet
  a person who writes poems.

poetry
  words written in lines of a certain length and often rhyming at the ends.

point
  1 the sharp end.
  2 to show with a finger.
  3 a dot.
  4 a place or time.

poison
  something that can kill or harm you if it gets into your body.

poisonous
  containing poison.

poke
  to push with a stick, a finger or a rod.

polar bear
  a large, white bear which lives near the North Pole.

pole
  a long, rounded stick, a rod.

police
  people who make sure that the law is obeyed.

polish
  1 to make smooth and bright by rubbing.
  2 a powder, paste or liquid used for polishing.

polite
  well-behaved, well-mannered.

pollen
  a kind of fine dust found in flowers.

polythene
  a kind of plastic.

pond
  a small lake.

pony
  a kind of small horse.

polar bears

polish

pond

ABCDEFGHIJKLMNOPQRSTUVWXYZ

poodle

poodle
a kind of dog kept as a pet.

pool
1 a small pond.
2 a pond prepared for swimming.

poor
1 not having much money, not rich.
2 not very good.

pop
1 a sudden, soft noise.
2 a kind of modern music, especially popular with young people.

poppy
a kind of plant with large flowers, often red.

popular
well-liked by people.

porch
a shelter over an outside door of a building.

pork
meat from a pig.

porpoise
a sea animal rather like a dolphin.

porridge
a breakfast food made of oatmeal boiled in water or milk.

port
1 a place where ships land their cargo.
2 the left-hand side of a ship as you face forward.

portrait
a picture of a person.

position
1 the place where something or somebody is.
2 a job.

positive
certain, quite sure.

possible
able to be done; likely to take place.

poppy

porch

porpoise

a b c d e f g h i j k l m n o p q r s t u v w x y z

post

post
1 an upright pole fixed in the ground.
2 the system for sending and getting letters.
3 a job, a position.

poster
a large piece of paper with a message on it which is put up in public places.

postman
the person who collects and delivers letters and parcels.

pot
1 a round container, for example a **teapot**.
2 a deep container with a handle for cooking.

potato
an oval or round vegetable which grows under the ground.

pottery
pots and dishes made of baked clay.

pouch
a small bag.

pound
1 an amount of British money equal to 100 pence.
2 a measure of weight.
3 to beat very hard.

pour
1 to make liquid flow out of a container.
2 to rain heavily.

powder
dust made by crushing a hard material.

power
strength, force.

practice
doing something often in order to become better at it.

practise
to do something often in order to become better at it.

signpost

postman

pour

praise

praise
to say good things about a person or thing.

pram
a small carriage for a baby or a doll.

prawn
a kind of small shellfish.

pray
to speak to God.

prayer
what you say when praying.

preach
to give a religious talk.

precious
very valuable, greatly loved.

prefer
to like one person or thing more than the others.

prepare
to make or get ready.

present
1 a gift.
2 in a place or with people.

present
to hand something over to someone else.

presently
in a short time, soon.

preserve
to keep something from harm or from going bad.

president
the head of a country or of an organisation.

press
1 to push hard.
2 to make smooth with an iron.

pretend
1 to act as though you are somebody or something else.
2 to act as though something is true, which is not.

prawns

present

press

pretty

pretty
attractive, delightful to see.

prey
a bird or animal that is hunted.

price
what you must pay to buy something, the cost.

priceless
very valuable.

prick
to make a small hole with something pointed.

prickly
1 having sharp points or thorns like a holly leaf.
2 bad tempered, easily annoyed.

pride
the feeling or belief that you are better than other people in some way.

priest
someone who performs religious ceremonies.

prim
neat; easily shocked; almost too well-behaved.

primary
first; earliest.

prime minister
the head of a government.

primrose
a kind of small, yellow spring flower.

prince
a man or boy in a royal family.

princess
a woman or girl in a royal family.

principal
most important, chief, head.

print
1 to press letters onto paper by a machine.
2 to write without joining up the letters.

price

prickly

primrose

A B C D E F G H I J K L M N O P Q R S T U V W X Y Z

prison

prison
a place where people who have broken the law are kept.

private
belonging to one person or group only.

prize
a reward for winning something.

probably
likely.

problem
a difficult thing to work out.

procession
an orderly march.

prod
to poke (with a stick, for example).

pro<u>d</u>uce
1 to bring out; to show.
2 to make.

pro<u>d</u>uce
something produced by growing.

profit
gain, money that you make when you sell something for more than you paid for it.

program
a number of instructions for a computer which you use to tell it what to do.

programme
1 a list of performers and information about what will happen (for example, at a concert or competition).
2 something broadcast on television or radio.

project
1 a plan for something special.
2 a long piece of work (for example, finding information about a subject).

promise
to say firmly that you will do something.

prompt
in good time, at the right time.

prong
the sharp spike of a fork.

private

pro<u>d</u>uce

prongs

a b c d e f g h i j k l m n o p q r s t u v w x y z 161

pronounce

pronounce
to say a word in a certain way.

proof
what shows or proves something to be true.

propeller
curved blades on a ship or an aeroplane which drive it forward.

proper
correct, right.

property
something which belongs to someone.

protect
to prevent someone or something being harmed or damaged.

protest
to say strongly that you are against something.

proud
thinking very well of yourself or something you own.

prove
to show that something is true.

proverb
a short, well-known saying.

provide
to give what is needed, to supply.

prune
a dried plum.

psalm
a Bible poem or song.

public
1 for everybody to use.
2 in open view.

publish
to put into print for sale.

pudding
a sweet food eaten at the end of a meal.

puddle
a small pool of usually dirty water.

puff
a short burst of breath or smoke.

propeller

pudding

puddle

ABCDEFGHIJKLMNOPQRSTUVWXYZ

puffin

puffin
 a kind of sea bird with a short, thick beak.

pull
 to drag something towards you.

pullover
 a piece of clothing for the upper part of the body.

pulse
 the beating of the heart.

pump
 1 to force air or liquid into or along something.
 2 a machine which does this.

punch
 1 to hit with the fist.
 2 to make a hole in something.

punctual
 arriving at the exact time.

puncture
 a small hole made by something pointed.

punish
 to make someone suffer for something bad they have done wrong.

pupil
 a person who is being taught, especially in a school.

puppet
 a kind of doll which can be made to move (by pulling strings, for example).

puppy
 a young dog.

pure
 with nothing added.

purple
 a colour made by mixing red and blue.

purr
 the noise made by a cat when it is pleased.

purse
 a small bag for holding money.

push
 to press against something to try to move it.

pump

puncture

push

a b c d e f g h i j k l m n o p q r s t u v w x y z 163

pushchair

pushchair
a small pram like a chair.

put
to move something into a place.

putty
a soft mixture which hardens to hold glass in a frame, for example.

puzzle
1 something which is difficult to understand.
2 a game which has to be worked out.

pyjamas
trousers and a jacket top which are worn in bed.

pylon
a metal tower used to hold up electric cables.

python
a large snake which squeezes its victims to death.

pushchair

python

pylon

Q q

quack
the noise made by ducks.
quality
how good or bad something is.
quantity
an amount.
quarrel
to disagree angrily with someone.
quarry
1 a place where stone is taken out of the ground.
2 an animal that is being hunted.
queen
1 a woman who is the ruler of a country.
2 the wife of a king.
queer
strange, odd, peculiar.
question
something that needs an answer.
queue (say 'Q')
a line of waiting people or vehicles.
quick
fast, at great speed, done in a short time.
quiet
with no sound or very little, not loud.
quilt
a cover for a bed filled with feathers or other soft material.
quite
1 completely, fully.
2 a little, but not very.
quiver
1 to shake, to tremble.
2 a holder for arrows.
quiz
a game in which a lot of questions have to be answered.

quarry

queue

quick

a b c d e f g h i j k l m n o p q r s t u v w x y z

Rr

rabbit
   a small, furry animal with long ears and long back legs which lives in holes in the ground.

race
   1 a test of speed.
   2 people of the same kind or colour.

rack
   a frame or bar for holding things.

racket
   1 a kind of bat used in some sports (tennis, for example).
   2 a lot of very loud noise.

radar
   a way of helping to guide ships and aeroplanes by using radio waves.

radiator
   1 a device that sends out heat.
   2 the front part of the engine of a motor car which cools the engine.

raffia
   material made from the leaf stems of a palm tree and used to weave mats and baskets, for example.

raffle
   a game of chance used to make money. Tickets with numbers are sold and some numbers win prizes.

raft
   a platform, often of logs, made to float on water.

rag
   a piece of old or torn cloth.

rage
   great anger, a violent temper.

raid
   a sudden, unexpected attack.

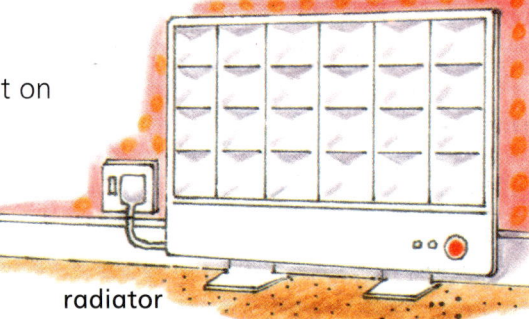

rackets

radar

radiator

rail

rail
a fixed wooden, plastic or metal bar (for example, for hanging things on).

railway
1 the rails on which trains run.
2 anything to do with trains.

rain
drops of water falling from the clouds.

rainbow
an arch of coloured stripes sometimes seen in the sky in rainy weather.

raise
1 to lift, to move up.
2 to bring up (a family or animals).
3 to collect (money).

raisin
a dried grape.

rake
a garden tool with spikes (for scratching the earth or gathering dead leaves, for example).

ram
1 a male sheep.
2 to crash into.

ramble
1 a long country walk.
2 to talk foolishly and without thinking.

ramp
a slope between two different levels.

ranch
a large cattle or sheep farm.

rank
1 a line or row (of soldiers, for example).
2 a person's official position (for example, a captain in the army).

ransom
a sum of money to buy a prisoner's freedom.

rap
a sharp blow or knock.

rapid
very fast, very quick.

railway

ramble

ramp

a b c d e f g h i j k l m n o p q **r** s t u v w x y z   167

rare

rare
scarce, not often seen.
rascal
1 a very wicked person.
2 a badly-behaved child.
rash
1 not thinking enough, doing things too quickly.
2 a large number of spots on the skin.
raspberry
a kind of juicy, red berry.
rat
an animal like a large mouse.
rate
1 the speed of something.
2 the price which has been fixed.
rattle
1 the noise of things being shaken together.
2 a baby's toy that rattles.
raven
a large, black bird of the crow family.
raw
1 not cooked.
2 cold and wet.
ray
a beam or shaft of light.
razor
a very sharp tool for shaving the skin.
reach
1 to stretch and touch.
2 to arrive at, to get to.
read
to understand the meaning of written or printed words.
ready
1 willing to do something.
2 prepared for use.
real
true, not false.
realise
to come to understand something.

raven

razor

reach

really

really
truly.
reap
to cut and gather in a crop.
rear
1 the back part.
2 (of a horse) to stand up on the hind legs.
3 to look after children or small animals until they are fully grown.
reason
the explanation, the cause.
reasonable
not asking too much.
rebel
to turn against a leader and stop obeying orders.
rebel
a person who rebels.
receipt
a paper stating that something has been received.
receive
to take, to get something that is given or sent.
recent
just happened.
recipe
a list of instructions telling you how to cook something.
recite
to say aloud from memory.
record
1 a disc for playing music or words on a **record-player**.
2 the best that has been done so far (for example, in a sport).
3 something written down to tell you what has happened.
record
1 to copy (voices or music) on a disc or tape.
2 to write down.

rear

receipt

record

recorder

recorder
a wooden musical instrument played by blowing.

recover
1 to get better after an illness.
2 to get something back.

re-cover
to put a new cover on.

rectangle
a flat shape like the shape of this page.

red
the colour of blood.

reduce
to make something less or smaller.

reed
a kind of long, thin plant which grows near water.

reef
a line of rocks just below the level of the sea.

reel
1 a cylinder used for winding something onto (for example, a **fishing reel**, a **reel of cotton**).
2 a lively Scottish dance.
3 to stagger about.

referee
the person who makes sure that a game is played fairly.

reference book
a book in which one can look things up, such as a dictionary or an atlas.

reflect
1 to show or shine back, like a mirror.
2 to think.

refreshment
something to eat or drink.

refrigerator
a special kind of container for keeping food cold.

refuse
rubbish.

fishing reel

reflect

refuse

refuse
   not to accept; to say 'No'.
regiment
   a large group of soldiers, a part of an army.
region
   a part of the world or of a country.
regret
   to be very sorry about.
regular
   happening often at the same time; usual.
rehearse
   to practise something such as a play or concert.
reign
   1 to rule as a king or queen.
   2 the length of time a king or queen reigns.
reindeer
   a kind of deer with long horns which lives in cold, northern countries.
reins
   straps used to control and guide a horse, for example.
relation
   someone in the same family.
relative
   someone in the same family.
relay
   a race in which each person in a team runs or swims a different part of the course.
reliable
   able to be trusted.
relief
   1 the feeling when pain, fear or worry stops.
   2 help for people in trouble.
religion
   a way of believing in God or in gods.
religious
   to do with religion; following a religion.

region

reins

relatives

remain

remain
  to stay behind.

remark
  something said about someone or something.

remarkable
  worth noting.

remedy
  a cure.

remember
  to bring back into the mind; not to forget.

remind
  to make someone remember.

removal
  moving from one house to another.

remove
  1 to take away.
  2 to move from one place to another.

rent
  the money you pay to use something which belongs to someone else.

repair
  to mend, to put right.

repeat
  to do or say something again.

replace
  to put back.

reply
  to answer.

report
  a description of something which has happened.

reptile
  an animal with cold blood such as a snake or lizard.

request
  to ask politely for something.

require
  to need, to want.

rescue
  to save, to take out of danger.

remove

repair

rescue

reserve

reserve
 1 to keep something until it is needed.
 2 something spare or extra.
 3 an area of land set aside for wildlife.

reservoir
 a large lake which has been specially made to supply a town or city with water.

respect
 to admire, to look up to.

rest
 1 the others; what is left over.
 2 to be still, not to work or do anything tiring.

restaurant
 a place where you can buy food to eat there.

restore
 1 to give or bring back.
 2 to clean and repair.

result
 1 what happens because of something.
 2 the final score in a game.

retire
 to stop working, usually because you have reached a certain age.

return
 1 to go or come back to a place.
 2 to give back.

reveal
 to show, to make known (especially something hidden).

revenge
 the hurt you do to someone in return for something they did to you.

reverse
 1 to go backwards.
 2 to go in the opposite direction.

revolution
 a great change, especially a change in the government of a country, made by force.

revolver
 a kind of small handgun which can fire several bullets without being reloaded.

reserve

reservoir

reverse

abcdefghijk l m n o p q **r** s t u v w x y z 173

reward

reward
something you are given for something good or brave you have done.

rhinoceros
a large, thick-skinned wild animal with one or two horns on its nose, found mainly in Africa.

rhubarb
a garden plant with juicy stalks that can be eaten.

rhyme
1 word endings which sound alike.
2 a piece of poetry with rhymes in it.

rhythm
the steady beat or time of poetry or music.

rib
one of the bones across the chest.

ribbon
a narrow band of material (for tying things, for example).

rice
a plant grown in hot countries; the grain of this is an important food.

rich
1 having a lot of money or other valuable things.
2 (of food) having a lot of fat or sugar, for example.

rid
to be free of.

riddle
a word puzzle in which a question has a funny answer.

ride
1 to move about in a vehicle or on an animal.
2 a journey or trip on an animal or a vehicle.

ridiculous
so silly that it may be laughed at.

rifle
a kind of gun with a long barrel.

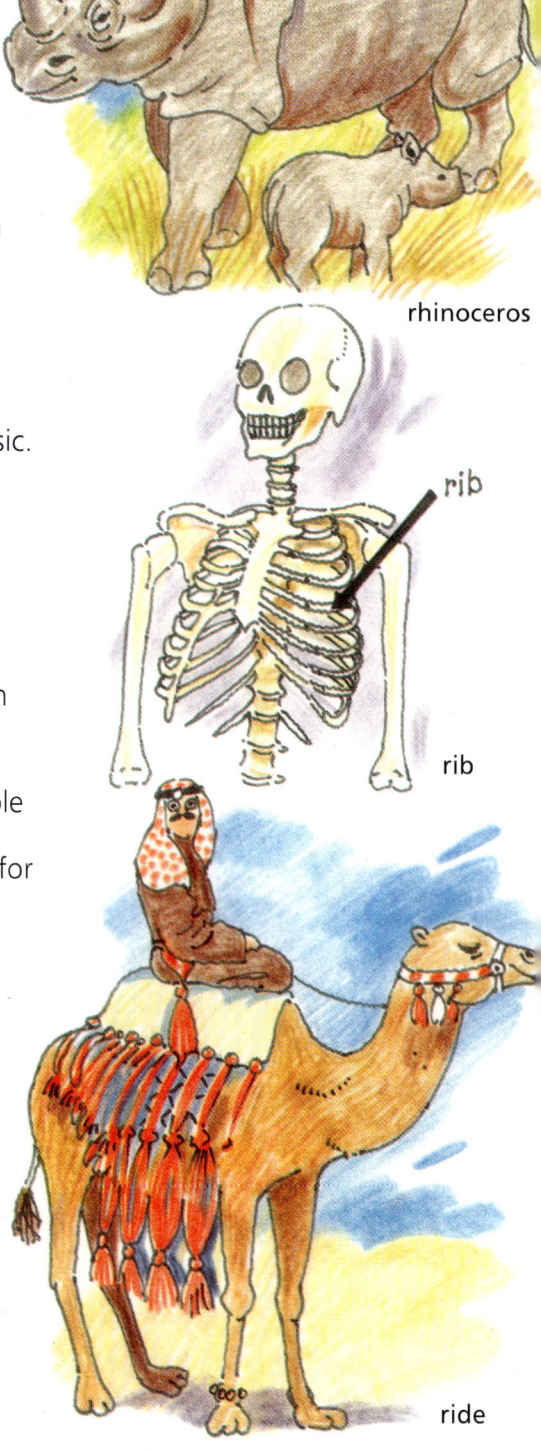

rhinoceros

rib

rib

ride

ABCDEFGHIJKLMNOPQ**R**STUVWXYZ

right

right
1 correct; not wrong.
2 good; true.
3 the opposite of left.

rim
the edge of something round, such as a bowl or a wheel.

ring
1 a round piece of metal (for example, one worn on the finger).
2 a circle.
3 the sound made by a bell.

rink
a place made specially for ice-skating or roller-skating.

rinse
to wash with clean water, usually after washing with soap.

rip
to tear roughly.

ripe
fully grown, ready to eat.

ripple
a tiny wave.

rise
1 to get up.
2 to go higher.

risk
the danger of something going wrong.

rival
a person who tries to equal or to do better than another person.

river
a long, wide stream of water, usually flowing into the sea.

road
a wide track on which vehicles can travel.

roam
to wander about.

roar
a loud, deep sound, the noise made by a lion or by thunder.

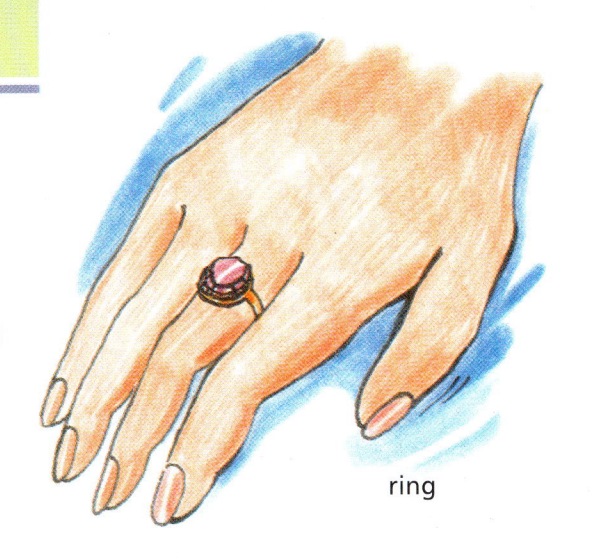

ring

ripple

roar

roast

roast
 to cook in fat in an oven or over a fire.

rob
 to take something that does not belong to you, to steal from.

robber
 a person who steals.

robe
 a long, loose piece of clothing.

robin
 a small, brown bird with a red breast.

robot
 a machine that can do some of the work a person can do.

rock
 1 stone; a large piece of it.
 2 to move from side to side.
 3 a long, sticky sweet shaped like a stick.
 4 a kind of popular music.

rockery
 part of a garden with lots of rocks, where certain plants grow well.

rocket
 1 a long tube driven into the air by gas or an explosion.
 2 a kind of firework.
 3 a spaceship.

rod
 a thin bar of wood or metal, for example.

rogue
 a wicked person that you cannot trust.

roll
 1 to turn over and over.
 2 something rolled into the shape of a cylinder.
 3 a long sound made by drums.
 4 a small piece of bread, like a small loaf.

roller skate
 wheels attached to a boot or shoe to allow you to move along quickly.

roof
 1 the top covering of a building.
 2 the top part of the inside of the mouth.

robin

rockery

roller skates

rook
1 a black bird of the crow family with a grey beak.
2 a chess piece, also called a castle.

room
1 a part of a building, with its own floor, walls and ceiling.
2 space for something.

root
1 the part of a plant which is in the soil and absorbs water to feed the plant.
2 the beginning or the origin of something (for example, the root of a problem).

roots

rope
a thick cord.

rose
a plant with large, bright flowers and thorns on its stem.

rosehip
the fruit of the rose bush.

rosy
pink in colour.

rot
to go bad (and die).

rotten
1 gone bad.
2 nasty, unpleasant.

rough
1 not smooth; coarse.
2 wild and stormy.

rough

round
the same shape as a ball or ring.

rounders
a game played by two sides with a bat and a ball.

route
the way to go somewhere.

row (rhymes with 'low')
1 to move a boat with oars.
2 a line of people or things.

row (rhymes with 'now')
a noisy quarrel.

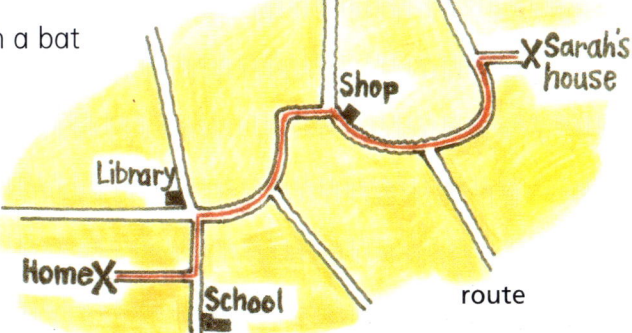

route

a b c d e f g h i j k l m n o p q **r** s t u v w x y z 177

rowing boat

rowing boat
   a boat driven by oars.

royal
   connected with kings and queens.

rub
   to move one thing against another many times.

rubber
   1 elastic material made from the sap of the rubber tree (used for making tyres, for example).
   2 a small piece of rubber or plastic used for rubbing out writing.

rubbish
   1 waste things that are of no use.
   2 nonsense.

ruby
   a deep-red precious stone.

rucksack
   a bag you can carry on your back.

rudder
   a piece of wood or metal fixed at the back to steer a boat or an aeroplane.

rude
   vulgar, not polite.

rug
   1 a small carpet, a mat.
   2 a kind of blanket, sometimes used to keep the knees warm when sitting down.

rugby
   a game played with an oval ball which may be kicked or carried.

ruin
   1 a building which has fallen down.
   2 to wreck; to spoil.

rule
   1 a law that must be followed.
   2 to have power over other people.

ruler
   1 a person who rules.
   2 a strip of wood or other material used for measuring or drawing straight lines.

rubber

rucksack

ruler

rumble

rumble
a deep roll of sound like the sound of thunder.

rumour
something you hear which may or may not be true.

run
to move very quickly on foot.

rung
a step on a ladder.

rush
1 to move very quickly; to hurry.
2 a kind of long, thin plant which grows near water.

rust
a reddish-brown coating sometimes found on iron and steel.

rustle
a gentle rubbing sound, like paper being moved.

rusty
covered with rust.

rung

rung

rush

rusty

S s

sabbath
: the day for the worship of God in the Jewish and Christian religions.

sack
: 1 a large, very strong bag, usually made of rough cloth.
: 2 to remove somebody from a job.

sad
: unhappy, miserable.

saddle
: the seat of a bicycle; a seat for the rider of a horse.

safari
: a journey in Africa to see wild animals or to hunt them.

safari park
: a park where you can see wild animals roaming about.

safe
: 1 not in danger, free from possible harm.
: 2 a strong, locked metal box used to keep valuable things in.

safety belt
: a seat belt.

sag
: to hang or bend downwards, often in the middle.

sail
: 1 a large piece of strong cloth used on a sailing boat to make it move in the wind.
: 2 to travel in a boat.

sailor
: 1 a person who works on a ship.
: 2 a person who sails a yacht.

saint
: a very good and holy person.

saddle

sag

sail

180 A B C D E F G H I J K L M N O P Q R S T U V W X Y Z

salad

salad
   a dish of vegetables, eaten cold and usually raw.

sale
   1 the selling of things.
   2 a time when things are sold at a lower price than usual.

saliva
   the liquid in your mouth.

salmon
   a kind of large fish with pink flesh.

salt
   a mineral used to flavour or preserve food.

salute
   to greet, especially by raising the hand to the forehead.

same
   not different; exactly like.

sample
   1 a small piece to show what something is like.
   2 to test, to try out.

sand
   tiny grains of stone or shells often found at the seaside or in the desert.

sandal
   an open-topped shoe fastened with straps or cords.

sandwich
   two slices of bread with a filling between them.

sane
   not mad; sensible.

sap
   1 the liquid in the stems of plants and trees.
   2 to weaken, to drain energy from something.

sarcastic
   being hurtful to someone by saying something but meaning the opposite.

sardine
   a small sea-fish used as food.

sale

salmon

sandwich

a b c d e f g h i j k l m n o p q r s t u v w x y z

sash

sash
1 a long, wide ribbon worn round the waist or over the shoulder.
2 a window frame.

satchel
a child's schoolbag.

satellite
a natural or man-made body moving in space round a planet.

satin
a kind of smooth cloth with one shiny side, usually made of silk.

satisfy
to make content and happy.

satsuma
a kind of fruit like a small orange.

sauce
a thick liquid food eaten with other food to add flavour.

saucepan
a metal container with a handle used for cooking.

saucer
a small, round plate on which a cup stands.

sausage
a mixture of minced meat and other things in a thin skin.

savage
fierce, wild, cruel.

save
1 to help someone to be safe.
2 to keep something till you need it.
3 to use less of something.

savings
money you save up.

saw
a metal cutting-tool with sharp, pointed teeth.

say
to speak, to tell in words.

scab
a hard covering which forms over a wound or spot.

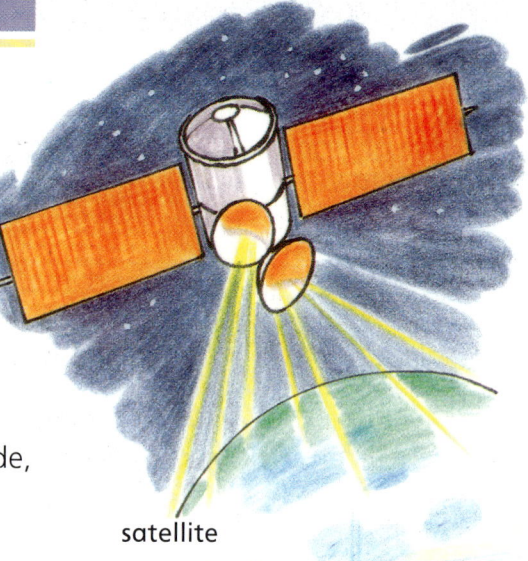

satellite

saucepan

savings

scabbard

scabbard
a sheath or cover for a sword or dagger.
scald
to burn with hot liquid.
scale
1 a set of numbers or marks for measuring.
2 a set of musical notes going up and down.
3 a small piece of flat, shiny material on the skin of a fish or snake, for example.
scales
a machine for weighing things.
scalp
the skin and hair on the top of the head.
scamper
to run quickly and lightly.
scar
a mark left on the skin by a wound.
scarce
not often found because there are not many.
scare
to frighten badly.
scarf
a length of cloth used as a covering for the neck and shoulders.
scarlet
a very bright red colour.
scatter
1 to throw something about in different directions.
2 to move away quickly in different directions.
scene
1 a view.
2 a part of a play.
3 the place where something happened.
scent
1 a pleasant smell, a perfume.
2 the smell an animal leaves behind it.
scheme
a plan.

scabbard

scarf

scatter

a b c d e f g h i j k l m n o p q r **s** t u v w x y z   183

school

school
1 a place where people, usually children, go to learn.
2 a large group of fish swimming together.

science
knowledge of and learning about nature and how things are made.

scientist
a person who studies science.

scissors
a cutting tool with two blades fastened together in the middle.

scold
to talk harshly to someone because they have done something wrong.

scorch
to singe, to burn something slightly, often making it brown.

score
1 to count points, runs or goals in a game or competition.
2 the number of points, runs or goals made in a game or competition.

scout
a person who is sent out to find out information (about an enemy, for example).

scowl
to give a very angry look, to frown.

scramble
1 to climb or crawl quickly, often over rough ground.
2 to mix up.

scrap
1 a tiny piece.
2 rubbish thrown away.
3 a fight.

scrape
1 to rub and clean with something hard.
2 a difficulty.

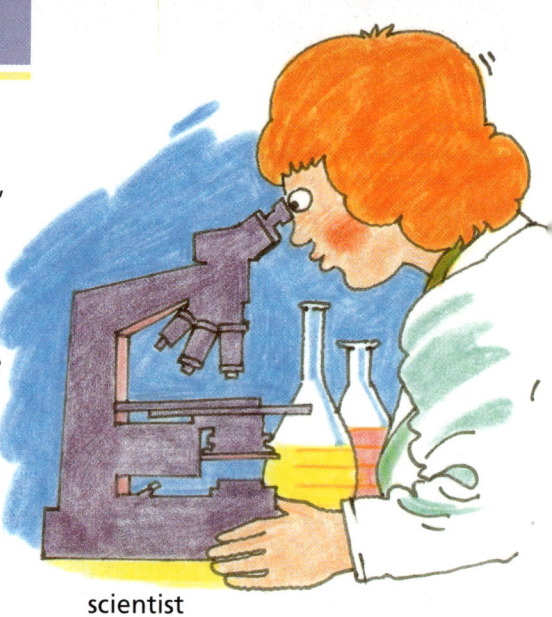

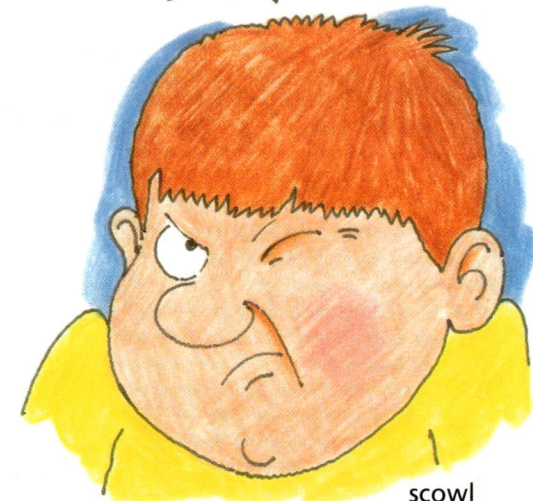

scientist

scissors

scowl

scratch

scratch
1 to mark or tear slightly with something sharp or pointed.
2 to rub the skin because it is itchy.

scrawl
to write badly, to scribble.

scream
to make a piercing cry, usually because of fear or pain.

screech
a harsh, high sound.

screen
1 a large, white surface on which a film is shown; the front viewing part of a television set or computer.
2 a large, covered frame (for example, used as shelter from the cold or to divide up a room).

screw
a nail with grooves round it so that it can be turned by a **screwdriver**.

scribble
to write so quickly and carelessly that the writing can hardly be read.

scrub
to clean with water and, usually, a brush.

scuffle
a struggle with much pushing, a kind of fight.

sculptor
a person who makes sculpture.

sculpture
artistic shapes made out of stone, metal or other materials.

sea
the salt water which surrounds the land on the earth's surface.

seal
1 a kind of sea animal.
2 a design used as the special badge of an important organisation, often stamped into wax.
3 to close or fasten tightly (an envelope, for example).

screens

screwdriver

screw

a b c d e f g h i j k l m n o p q r **s** t u v w x y z

seam

seam
1 a line of stitches where cloth is joined.
2 a layer of coal, for example, under the ground.

search
1 to look very hard in order to find something.
2 **search for** to look for.

seasick
feeling sick because of the movement of a boat or ship.

season
1 one of the four main parts of the year: spring, summer, autumn, winter.
2 a special time of the year (for example, the **festive season**).
3 to add something to food to give it more flavour.

seat
something to sit on.

seat belt
a belt you wear in a car to stop you being thrown about if there is an accident.

seaweed
plants which grow in the sea.

second
1 after the first.
2 a very short period of time. There are 60 seconds in a minute.

secondary school
a school for children between the ages of 11 and 18.

second-hand
not new, already owned by somebody else.

secret
something known only to a few people.

secretary
a person whose job it is to write letters and make arrangements for another person or for an organisation.

section
a part of something.

seasons

seaweed

see

see
1 what you are able to do with your eyes.
2 to understand.

seed
a grain from which a plant grows.

seek
to search for, to look for.

seem
to appear to be.

seesaw
a plank on which children sit at opposite ends and go up and down.

seize
to take hold of roughly; to grab quickly.

seldom
not often; rarely.

select
to choose; to pick out.

selection
a number of things that have been chosen.

selfish
thinking only about yourself.

sell
to give something to someone else in exchange for money.

send
to make someone or something go somewhere.

senior
1 older than others.
2 having a higher position in an organisation or having been there longer.

sense
1 the ability to think in a reasonable way.
2 the power to see, hear, smell, taste or touch.
3 a meaning.

sensible
having good sense.

sell

see

hear

smell

taste

touch

senses

a b c d e f g h i j k l m n o p q r **s** t u v w x y z 187

sentence

sentence
1 a group of words that make sense together.
2 a punishment given by a judge at the end of a trial.

sentry
a soldier on guard at a door or gate.

separate
divided, not joined to something else.

sergeant (say 'sarjent')
an officer in the police or in the army.

serial
a story told or written in parts.

serious
1 of great importance.
2 causing great harm (for example, an illness, a crime).
3 not cheerful or funny.

servant
someone who does work for another person, especially work in the other person's house.

serve
1 to work for someone.
2 to give out goods in a shop.
3 to give food to.

service
1 something you do for others.
2 something people can use to help them (for example, a **bus service**).
3 a ceremony in church.

set
1 to put something in a place.
2 a group of people or things which are alike in some way.

settee
a couch, a sofa.

settle
1 to sink to the bottom.
2 to become still or calm.
3 to go to live in a place for a long time.
4 to fix, to decide on.

sergeant

service

settee

A B C D E F G H I J K L M N O P Q R **S** T U V W X Y Z

several

several
some, a few, not many.

severe
very serious or bad (for example, an illness or a frost).

sew (say 'so')
to join together with stitches using a needle and thread.

sex
one of the two groups, male and female, that people and animals belong to.

shabby
almost worn out.

shade
1 a place where there is shelter from the sun or other strong light.
2 the depth of a colour, its lightness or darkness.

shadow
1 a dark part where something is keeping out the light.
2 a dark shape seen where something comes between the light and another surface.

shaft
1 the long handle of a spade, an axe or a golf club.
2 the long part of an arrow or a spear.
3 a long space going up or down (for example, into a mine).

shake
to move quickly from side to side or up and down, often because of cold or fear, to shiver.

shallow
not deep.

shame
a feeling of being unhappy because you have done wrong.

shampoo
a liquid for washing the hair.

shape
the outline of something.

shadow

shallow

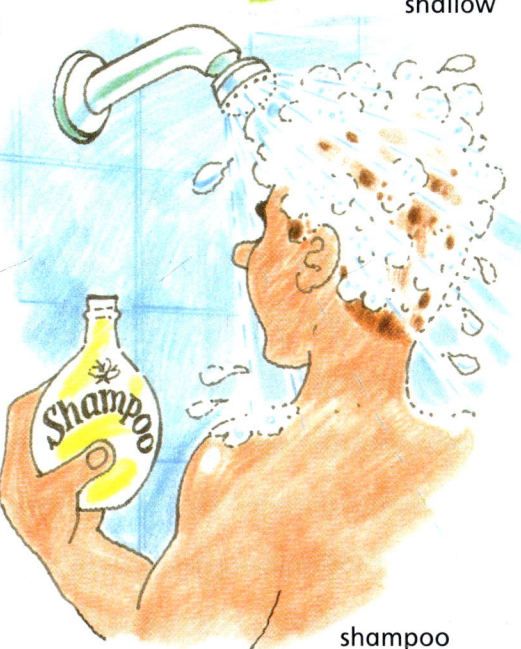

shampoo

share

share
1 to divide into parts.
2 to use something along with someone else.

shark
a large, sometimes dangerous, fish with sharp teeth.

sharp
1 pointed, able to cut, stab or stick into something.
2 quick, sudden.
3 able to think, see, hear well and quickly.
4 above the correct note in music.

shave
to remove hair from the skin with a razor.

shawl
a covering for the head and shoulders or for wrapping a baby.

sheaf
a bundle of things tied together, especially newly-cut corn.

shears
large scissors (used for cutting hedges or wool from sheep, for example).

shed
1 a hut.
2 to let fall or pour out (for example, tears, leaves).

sheep
an animal with a woollen coat, kept on farms.

sheet
1 a large piece of thin cloth often used on a bed.
2 a thin, flat piece of material such as paper, glass or metal.

shelf
a long, flat board fixed to a wall or cupboard, used for putting things on.

shell
1 the hard covering of an egg, nut, seed and of some creatures.
2 a large bullet.

share

shave

sheaf

shelter

shelter
    a place where you can be protected from bad weather or danger.

shepherd
    a person who looks after sheep.

shield
    1 to protect from harm.
    2 a large piece of metal or other material sometimes held by people to protect themselves when fighting.
    3 a prize in the shape of a shield.

shift
    to move.

shin
    the front of the leg between the knee and the ankle.

shine
    1 to give out light.
    2 to look bright, to sparkle.

ship
    a very large boat.

shipwreck
    the destruction of a ship, often in a storm.

shirt
    a piece of clothing for the upper part of the body, with sleeves and a collar, often worn by men.

shiver
    to shake because of cold or fear.

shoal
    a large group of fish of the same kind swimming together.

shock
    1 a sudden, violent surprise or force.
    2 to make someone feel shock.

shoe
    a covering for the foot.

shoot
    1 to fire a weapon.
    2 a new growth on a plant.
    3 to move very quickly.

shop
    a place where things are sold.

shield

shipwreck

shoal

shopping

shopping
things that you buy in a shop.

shore
the land along the edge of the sea or of a lake.

short
small from end to end, not long, not tall.

shorts
short trousers, with legs stopping above the knee.

shot
the shooting of a gun.

shoulder
the place where the arm joins the body.

shout
to speak or cry out in a loud voice.

shove
to push hard.

shovel
a tool for lifting loose things (for example, coal).

show
1 to allow to see.
2 where special things can be seen.

shower
1 a short fall of rain or snow.
2 a place to wash yourself where water sprays down on you from above.

shriek
a high-pitched scream of pain, surprise or laughter.

shrill
(of a sound) high-pitched.

shrimp
a very small kind of shellfish.

shrink
to become smaller.

shrub
a small tree or bush.

shudder
to shake violently with fear or cold.

shore

shorts

shovel

192

shut

shut
   1 not open, closed.
   2 to close.

shy
   afraid to speak; easily frightened.

sick
   1 feeling that you will bring up food from the stomach.
   2 ill, not well.

side
   1 the part at the edge of something.
   2 a team at games.

sieve
   an instrument with very small holes which lets only liquid and fine grains through.

sigh
   to make a low sound with a deep breath because you are tired, sad or bored.

sight
   1 being able to see.
   2 something seen.

sign
   1 a mark, movement or message which has a meaning.
   2 to write your name on.

signal
   a sign, sound or light which tells you something (for example, a red light telling you to stop).

signature
   a person's name written by himself or herself (for example, at the end of a letter).

silent
   quiet, still, without noise; not saying anything.

silk
   a kind of smooth, soft cloth.

silly
   foolish, stupid, not sensible.

silver
   a valuable, whitish metal (used to make jewellery, coins, spoons and forks, for example).

sieve

road signs

signal

a b c d e f g h i j k l m n o p q r s t u v w x y z

simple

simple
　1 plain, without any decoration.
　2 easy.

sin
　doing something very bad, which is against the laws of your religion.

sincere
　meaning what you say, honest.

sing
　to make music with the voice.

singe
　to burn slightly.

single
　1 only one.
　2 not married.

sink
　1 to go down slowly, especially in water.
　2 a fixed basin with taps and a drain.

sip
　to drink in tiny amounts.

sir
　1 a title given to a man.
　2 a polite title used in speaking to a man.

sister
　a girl or woman who has the same parents as another person.

sit
　to rest on your bottom with your back upright.

size
　how big something is.

skate
　1 a metal blade fitted to a boot to allow you to move quickly on ice.
　2 to move on ice using skates.
　3 to move on roller skates.

skateboard
　a flat board on wheels on which you can stand and move about for fun.

skeleton
　all the bones in the body.

sketch
　to draw quickly and roughly.

sing

sink

skateboard

A B C D E F G H I J K L M N O P Q R S T U V W X Y Z

ski

ski
1 a long thin piece of wood, plastic or metal fitted to a boot to allow you to move quickly over snow.
2 to move on snow using skis.

skid
to slide out of control on a slippery surface.

skill
cleverness, the ability to do something well.

skin
the outer covering of a person or animal or of a fruit or vegetable.

skinny
very thin.

skip
1 to move with little jumping steps.
2 to jump over a turning rope.

skipper
the captain of a ship or a team.

skirt
a piece of woman's clothing that hangs from the waist.

skittle
a wooden block knocked down by rolling or throwing a ball in the game of **skittles**.

skull
the bones that cover your head.

sky
the space above the earth where the sun, moon and stars are seen.

slab
a thick, flat piece of something.

slack
1 loose.
2 careless, not working hard.

slam
to bang or shut loudly.

slant
a slope.

slap
a hard smack with the flat of the hand.

skill

skirt

sky

a b c d e f g h i j k l m n o p q r s t u v w x y z

slate

slate
1 a kind of grey rock with splits easily into thin pieces.
2 a piece of this used as a tile on a roof.

slave
a person who is owned by another person and is forced to work for them without pay.

sledge
a small vehicle without wheels which will move smoothly on snow.

sleep
to rest with the eyes closed and without being conscious.

sleet
snow and rain falling together.

sleeve
the part of a piece of clothing that covers an arm.

slice
a thin piece cut from something larger.

slide
1 to move smoothly along a slippery surface; to slip.
2 a hair fastener.
3 a small photograph for showing on a screen.

slight
1 thin, small, not very strong.
2 small, of no importance.

slim
1 thin.
2 to become thinner.

sling
a bandage to support a broken arm.

slip
1 to move quickly and quietly.
2 to lose your balance on a smooth surface.
3 to make a mistake.
4 a piece of paper.

slippers
light, soft shoes worn in the house.

slate

sleep

slip

slippery

slippery
 so smooth that you are likely to slide on it.
slit
 a narrow cut or tear.
slope
 something that is higher at one end than at the other.
slow
 taking a long time, not quick.
slug
 a small animal like a snail, but without a shell.
slush
 half-melted, watery snow.
sly
 not to be trusted, crafty, cunning.
smack
 to hit with a flat hand.
small
 little, not big; not important.
smart
 1 clever, quick to understand.
 2 well-dressed.
 3 to have a stinging feeling.
smash
 to break into many pieces.
smear
 to spread something dirty, sticky or greasy over something.
smell
 1 to know about through your nose.
 2 to have a smell.
smile
 a happy look.
smoke
 1 the cloud which rises from something burning.
 2 to burn tobacco in a pipe or cigarette.
smooth
 flat, even, not rough.
smudge
 a dirty mark.

slope

slug

smoke

a b c d e f g h i j k l m n o p q r s t u v w x y z   197

smuggle

smuggle
 to take things secretly into a country without paying tax on them.

snack
 a small amount of food eaten between meals.

snail
 a small, soft animal with a shell on its back.

snake
 a smooth, legless animal which glides on its body.

snap
 1 to bite at something quickly.
 2 to break with a sharp noise.
 3 to make a sharp noise with the fingers.
 4 a photograph.

snare
 a trap set for animals.

snarl
 1 (of animals) to growl showing the teeth.
 2 to speak in an angry way.

snatch
 to grab quickly.

sneak
 1 to move secretly.
 2 a person who tells something bad about someone else secretly.

sneer
 to speak in a way that shows you do not think much of someone.

sneeze
 a sudden, noisy rush of air from the nose.

sniff
 to smell noisily with quick breaths.

snob
 a person who thinks too much about money and position.

snooker
 a game played on a special table with a cue and coloured balls.

snore
 to breathe heavily and noisily while asleep.

snack

snail

snore

snow

snow
> frozen water which falls in white flakes.

snug
> warm, cosy, comfortable.

soak
> 1 to make very wet.
> 2 to leave for a time in a liquid.

soap
> a fatty substance used with water for washing.

sob
> to weep noisily.

sock
> a cloth covering for your foot and ankle.

socket
> a hole into which something fits (for example, an electric plug).

sofa
> a couch, a settee.

soft
> 1 not hard.
> 2 gentle, mild, not rough.
> 3 quiet, not loud.

soil
> 1 the earth in which plants grow.
> 2 to make dirty.

soldier
> a person whose job it is to fight, a member of an army.

sole
> 1 the bottom of a foot or of a shoe or boot.
> 2 a kind of flat fish, used as food.

solemn
> very serious.

solid
> 1 hard, firm, not liquid or gas.
> 2 not hollow.

solo
> 1 a piece of music played or sung by one person alone.
> 2 done by one person alone (for example, a **solo** flight in an aeroplane).

socket

soil

sole

a b c d e f g h i j k l m n o p q r s t u v w x y z 199

solve

solve
to find the answer to.

somersault
to turn over and over, head over heels.

son
a male child of a parent.

song
a piece of music for the voice.

soon
in a short time.

soot
the black substance left behind after burning (for example, in a chimney).

sore
painful.

sorrow
a feeling of sadness.

sorry
feeling unhappy because of something you have done or something that has happened.

sort
1 a kind, a type.
2 to put into the right order (for example, putting things of the same size together).

sound
1 something you hear, a noise.
2 strong and healthy, in a good state.

soup
a food made by boiling vegetables, meat or fish in a lot of water.

sour
1 having a sharp, bitter taste like a lemon.
2 (of milk) not fresh.

south
the direction that is on the right as you face the rising sun.

souvenir
something you keep to remind you of something (for example, a place you visit).

sow (rhymes with 'low')
to put seeds into the ground so that they will grow.

solve

sorry

souvenir

space

space
1 the distance between things.
2 what is beyond the earth's atmosphere.

spaceship
a machine made to travel into space.

spade
1 a tool for digging soil.
2 a small spade shape on one of the four kinds of playing cards.

spanner
a tool which turns a metal nut to tighten or slacken it.

spare
1 not in use at present, extra.
2 to give up, to do without.

spark
a tiny piece of burning material.

sparkle
to shine with tiny movements of light.

sparrow
a kind of small, brown bird often seen near houses.

speak
to use the voice to say something, to talk.

spear
a weapon with a long, thin handle and a sharp point.

special
1 of a kind that is different.
2 made or done for one person or occasion.

speck
a tiny spot of something.

spectacles
glasses to help you to see better.

speech
speaking, the sounds you make when you speak.

speed
the quickness or slowness with which something is done.

spanner

sparrow

spectacles

a b c d e f g h i j k l m n o p q r **s** t u v w x y z   201

spell

spell
1 to arrange letters one by one to make words.
2 magic words.

spend
1 to give money to pay for something.
2 to use time in doing something.

sphere
a round ball, a globe.

spice
something, such as pepper, used to give food a special taste.

spider
a small, eight-legged creature which weaves a web to catch insects for food.

spike
a pointed object, especially of metal.

spill
to let a liquid or powder out of its container by accident.

spin
1 to turn round and round quickly.
2 to make cotton or wool, for example, into thread.

spinach
a kind of green vegetable.

spine
the backbone.

spire
the pointed, upper part of a tower, often of a church.

spirit
1 a ghost.
2 liveliness, energy.

spit
1 the liquid that forms in the mouth.
2 to force something out of your mouth.

splash
to throw or scatter liquid noisily.

splendid
1 excellent, very good.
2 very grand.

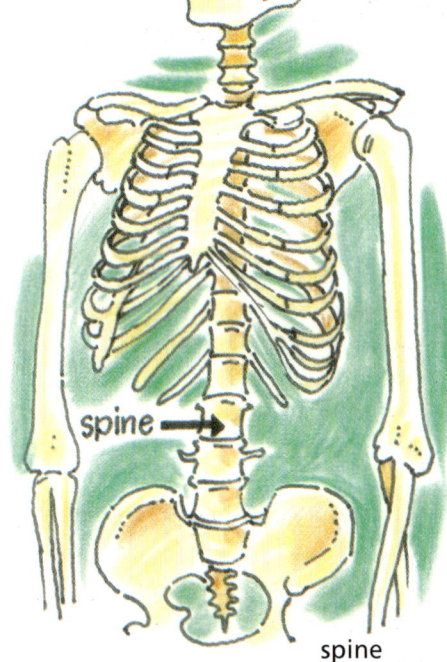

spin

spine

spine

splash

202 A B C D E F G H I J K L M N O P Q R **S** T U V W X Y Z

split

split
   to crack, to break something along its length.

spoil
   to ruin, to damage.

spoilt
   (of a child) having been given everything you want so that you become badly behaved.

spoke
   a thin bar from the centre to the rim of a wheel.

sponge
   1 a soft object which soaks up water, used for washing.
   2 a soft, light cake.

spoon
   an instrument used for eating or stirring soft foods or liquids.

sport
   games played for exercise or pleasure (for example, football or tennis).

spot
   1 a tiny mark.
   2 to notice.

spout
   a short tube through which a liquid is poured (for example, from a kettle or teapot).

sprain
   to injure by twisting badly (for example, the ankle or the wrist).

spray
   1 thin jets of water.
   2 a small bunch of flowers.

spread
   1 to take up more space.
   2 to scatter about.
   3 to cover a surface with something.

spring
   1 to jump in the air.
   2 a metal coil.
   3 a place where water appears from below the ground.
   4 the season between winter and summer.

spout

spread

spring

a b c d e f g h i j k l m n o p q r **s** t u v w x y z   203

sprinkle

sprinkle
  to scatter in small drops or grains.

sprint
  to run quickly for a short distance.

sprout
  to begin to grow.

spy
  a person who finds out and passes on information secretly.

squabble
  to quarrel noisily about small things.

square
  a shape like this □ with four equal sides.

squash
  to crush, to squeeze tightly together or into a small space.

squeak
  a small, sharp noise like that made by a mouse.

squeal
  a long, shrill cry, often caused by pain or joy.

squeeze
  1 to press together, to squash.
  2 to press to get something out (for example, an orange or a toothpaste tube).

squirm
  to twist about, to wriggle.

squirrel
  a small wild animal which has a bushy tail and lives among trees.

stab
  to make a wound with a sharp weapon.

stable
  a building where horses are kept.

stadium
  a large, open-air sports ground with rows of seats.

staff
  a group of people who work together (in an office or shop, for example).

sprint

squash

stable

stag

stag
  a male deer.

stage
  1 a platform in a theatre or hall where people act or dance, for example.
  2 a part of something (a journey, for example).

stagger
  to sway as you walk, to walk unsteadily.

stain
  a mark which spoils something.

stairs
  a set of steps leading to another floor in a building.

stairs

stale
  1 old, not fresh; no longer fit to eat.
  2 no longer interesting.

stalk
  1 the stem of a flower or plant.
  2 to track an animal quietly.

stall
  1 a counter for selling things (in a market, for example).
  2 a place where a single animal such as a cow or a horse is kept.
  3 **the stalls** seats on the ground level of a cinema or theatre.

stall

stammer
  to have difficulty in saying words, to repeat words without meaning to, to stutter.

stamp
  1 the little piece of paper stuck on a letter or parcel to show you have paid to have it sent through the post.
  2 to put your feet down hard and noisily.

stand
  1 to be in an upright position.
  2 to rise up.
  3 seats under cover at a sports ground.

standard
  a level of measurement or ability to be reached.

stand

a b c d e f g h i j k l m n o p q r s t u v w x y z 205

star

star
1 one of the tiny-looking bright objects that can be seen in the sky on a clear night.
2 a very famous person such as an actor or a singer.

starch
a white substance found in some foods such as bread or potatoes.

stare
to look at something steadily for a long time.

starling
a kind of small, noisy bird with dark, shiny feathers.

start
1 to begin.
2 to make a sudden movement.

startle
to surprise or frighten.

starve
to die or to be ill because you are without food.

state
1 the condition of a thing or person.
2 a country or its government.
3 a part of certain countries, such as the **United States of America**.
4 to say in words, either by writing or by speaking.

station
1 a place from which trains or buses begin or stop on a journey.
2 a place from which certain services are carried out (for example, a **police station** or a **fire station**).

statue
an image or likeness in wood or stone.

stay
not to go away, to remain.

steady
firm, not moving, not changing.

startle

fire station

statue

steak

steak
 a thick piece of meat or fish.

steal
 to take something that is not yours, to rob.

steam
 the mist or cloud that comes from boiling water.

steel
 a hard, strong metal which is made from iron.

steep
 sloping sharply.

steeple
 a pointed tower on top of a church.

steer
 to guide (a boat or a car, for example).

stem
 the thin part of a plant which holds the leaves or flowers.

step
 1 putting your foot forward or back in order to move.
 2 a flat place, in a stair or in front of a door, where you put your feet.

stepfather
 a man who marries your mother (for example, after your father dies).

stepmother
 a woman who marries your father (for example, after your mother dies).

stereo
 a machine for playing tapes and records, for example, which has two loudspeakers.

stern
 1 strict, harsh towards another person.
 2 the back part of a boat.

stew
 meat and vegetables cooked slowly in water.

stick
 1 a short, thin piece of wood.
 2 to fasten or be fastened by something such as glue.

steep

steeple

stick

sticky

sticky
　able to stick to something else.
stiff
　difficult to bend.
stile
　steps for climbing over a fence or wall.
still
　1 not moving, quiet, peaceful.
　2 the same now as before.
sting
　a sharp pain caused by an insect or plant.
stir
　to move something round and round with a stick or spoon.
stitch
　1 a loop made in sewing or knitting.
　2 a sudden pain in the side.
stocking
　a close-fitting covering for the leg and foot.
stomach
　the part of the body into which food goes after being eaten.
stone
　1 the hard material found on and below the surface of the earth; a small piece of this.
　2 a precious jewel.
　3 a hard seed found in some kinds of fruit.
　4 a measure of weight.
stool
　a seat without a back.
stop
　to end doing something.
store
　1 a place for keeping things.
　2 to save something for later.
　3 a large shop.
storey
　one floor of a building.
stork
　a kind of large bird with long legs and a very long, straight beak.

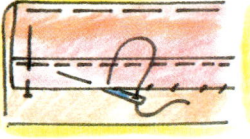

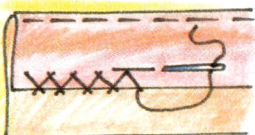

stile

hemming stitch　herringbone stitch

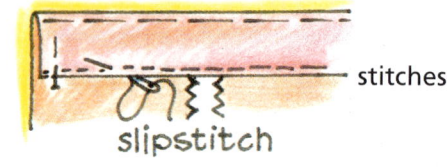

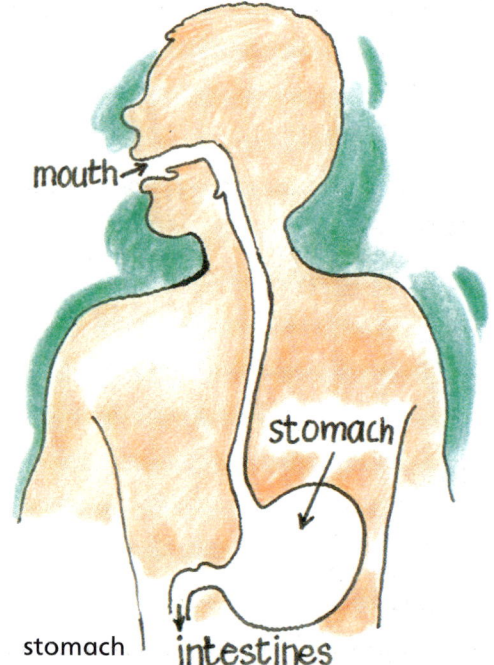

slipstitch — stitches

mouth

stomach

stomach　intestines

208　A B C D E F G H I J K L M N O P Q R **S** T U V W X Y Z

storm

storm
   rough weather with wind and rain.

story
   something that is told, especially about things that happen.

stout
   fat.

stove
   1 a cooker.
   2 a kind of closed fire for heating a room.

straight
   without a bend or turning.

strain
   1 to pull or try as hard as you can; to try too hard.
   2 to hurt a muscle.

strange
   unusual, different from the usual.

stranger
   1 a person you do not know.
   2 a person who does not know the district.

strap
   a long, thin piece of material (used to fasten things together, for example).

straw
   1 the dry stalks of wheat, barley or other grain.
   2 a thin tube for drinking through.

strawberry
   a kind of soft, red fruit which grows on small plants.

stray
   1 to wander away, to get lost.
   2 an animal which wanders because it has no home.

stream
   1 a small river.
   2 a number of people, animals or things moving steadily along.

street
   a road with buildings along its sides.

strap

strawberries

street

a b c d e f g h i j k l m n o p q r **s** t u v w x y z

strength

strength
being strong; power.

stretch
to make longer or wider by pulling.

stretcher
a frame to carry an injured or sick person lying down.

strict
1 firm, severe.
2 exact.

strike
1 to hit something hard.
2 (of a clock) to make a ringing sound.
3 when workers refuse to work.

string
thin cord.

strip
1 a long, narrow piece of something (for example, cloth or paper).
2 to undress; to uncover.

stroke
to pass the hand gently over something.

stroll
to walk along slowly.

strong
powerful, able to do difficult things with the body.

struggle
1 to fight, especially to get free of someone or something.
2 to try very hard to do something.

stubborn
not giving way easily, obstinate.

student
a person who is studying, especially in a college or university.

stuff
1 things, materials.
2 to fill something very full.

stumble
to fall or almost fall, especially by catching the foot on something.

stroke

struggle

student

210 A B C D E F G H I J K L M N O P Q R S T U V W X Y Z

stump

stump
1 the part of a tree which is left when the tree has been cut down.
2 one of three upright sticks used to bowl at in cricket.

stun
1 to amaze or shock someone.
2 to strike a person until he or she is unconscious.

stupid
having no sense, foolish, silly.

stutter
to stammer.

sty
1 a place where pigs are kept.
2 a small, painful swelling on the eyelid.

style
1 a way of doing, saying or making something.
2 a fashion.

submarine
a ship which can go along under water.

subtract
to take one thing away from another.

succeed
1 to manage to do what you try to do; to do well.
2 to come after, to follow.

suck
1 to take into the mouth by breathing inwards.
2 to move something, such as a sweet, about in your mouth without chewing it.

suddenly
happening without warning, all at once.

suffer
to feel great pain or sorrow.

sugar
a sweet substance.

suggest
to say what might be done, to hint.

stump

subtract

suck

suit

suit
1 a set of clothes (for example, a jacket with trousers or skirt).
2 to be good or right for, to fit.

suitable
correct, just right for something.

suitcase
a container with a handle and stiffened sides for carrying clothes and other belongings.

sulk
to show you are in a bad mood by not saying anything, to take the huff.

sum
1 something to be worked out with numbers.
2 to add numbers and find the total.

summer
the warmest season of the year, between spring and autumn.

sun
the large ball of fire in the sky which gives the earth light and heat.

supermarket
a large, self-service shop.

supersonic
faster than the speed of sound.

supper
a meal eaten in the evening.

supply
1 to provide the things that are needed.
2 a quantity or store of things.

support
1 to help someone by giving what is needed.
2 to hold up.
3 to provide for, especially by giving money.

suppose
to think; to believe something to be true.

sure
certain; not having any doubt.

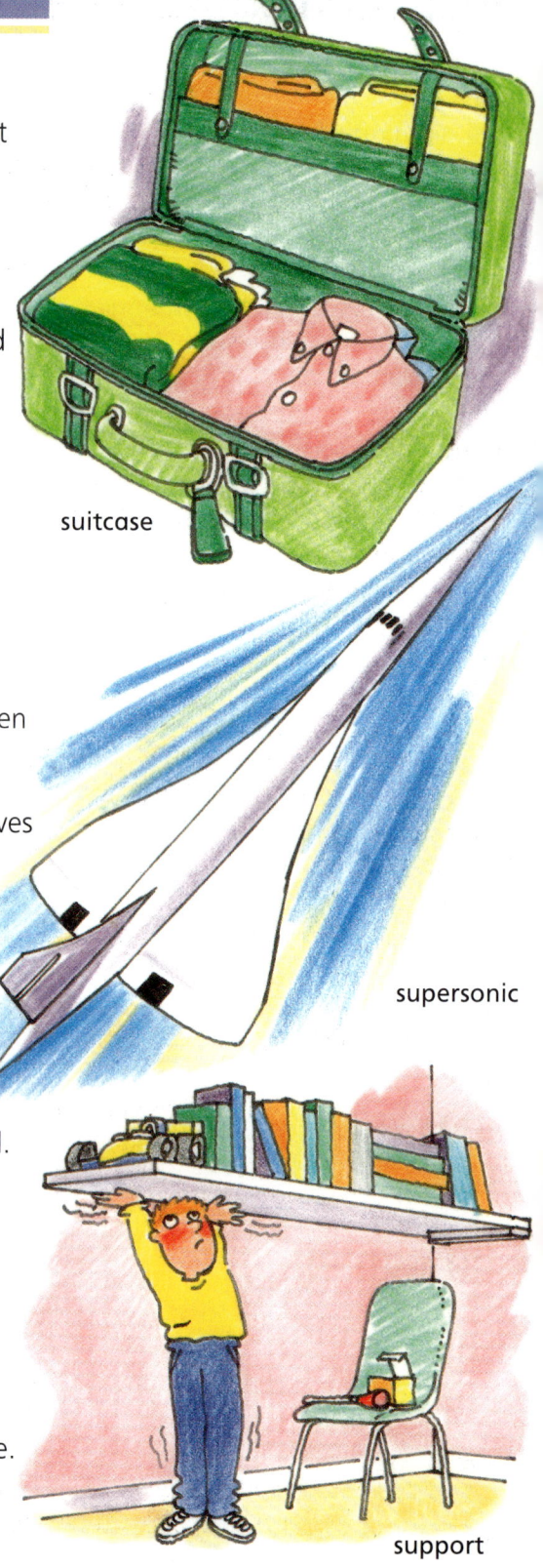

suitcase

supersonic

support

surface

surface
 1 the outside of something.
 2 the area at the top of something (for example, the top of water).

surgeon
 a doctor who carries out operations.

surgery
 a place where doctors and dentists work.

surname
 the family name, your last name.

surprise
 1 something you did not expect.
 2 the feeling that this causes, a shock.

surrender
 to give in, especially to an enemy.

surround
 to be all round.

swallow
 1 to take in through the throat.
 2 a kind of small bird with pointed wings and a long, forked tail.

swamp
 soft, wet ground, a marsh.

swan
 a kind of large, white water bird with a long neck.

swap
 to exchange.

swarm
 a large number of insects moving together.

sway
 to move from side to side.

swear
 1 to use bad words.
 2 to promise faithfully.

sweat
 liquid coming through the skin, when you are too hot.

sweater
 a piece of clothing, usually woollen, for the upper part of the body, a jersey.

surgeon

swamp

swarm

a b c d e f g h i j k l m n o p q r **s** t u v w x y z 213

sweep

sweep
   1 to clean somewhere with a brush.
   2 a person who cleans chimneys.

sweet
   1 pleasant to taste, like sugar, not sour.
   2 a small piece of sweet food, such as chocolate or a toffee.
   3 a sweet dish you eat at the end of a meal, a pudding.
   4 kind, charming, nice.

swell
   to become bigger.

swelling
   a part which becomes bigger, especially on the body.

swerve
   to move sideways quickly.

swift
   1 very fast, very speedy.
   2 a kind of small bird with long, narrow wings.

swim
   to move along in water by moving parts of the body.

swing
   1 to move backwards and forwards or round and round.
   2 a moving seat on ropes.
   3 a ride on a swing.

switch
   an instrument for turning electrical things on and off.

sword
   a metal weapon like a long, sharp knife with two sides.

sycamore
   a kind of tree with large leaves.

syrup
   sugar boiled in water to make a thick, sticky, sweet liquid.

swerve

swift

sycamore

Tt

tabby
1 a female cat.
2 a cat with greyish or brownish stripes.

table
1 a flat piece of furniture which stands on legs.
2 a list of numbers or facts put in order.

tablet
a pill of medicine.

tack
1 a small nail with a large head.
2 to fasten things together by using long stitches.
3 to change the direction of a sailing boat.

tackle
1 to try to do something.
2 to try to take the ball from another player (in football, for example).
3 the things which are necessary to do something (for example, **fishing-tackle**).

tadpole
a kind of small, black water animal which has a long tail and becomes a frog or toad.

tag
1 a label.
2 a children's chasing game.

tail
the part of a creature that sticks out at the back.

tailor
a person who makes clothes such as suits and coats.

take
1 to get hold of.
2 to carry away.
3 to swallow (medicine, for example).

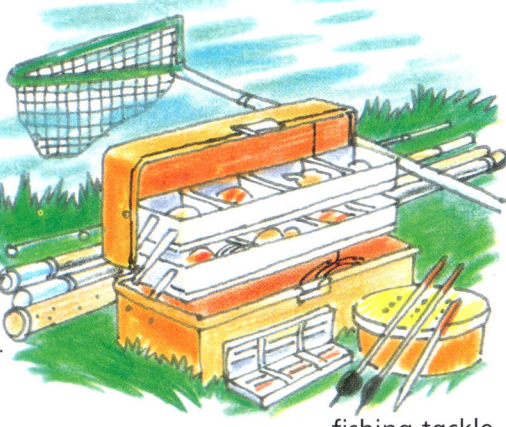

table

fishing-tackle

take

a b c d e f g h i j k l m n o p q r s t u v w x y z 215

tale

tale
a story.

talent
something a person is able to do well; an ability.

talk
to speak, to say something.

tall
bigger in height than usual.

tame
not wild; friendly; not exciting.

tan
1 a light-brown colour, especially the colour of your skin after you have been in the sun a lot.
2 to make animal skins into leather.

tangerine
a kind of small, sweet orange.

tangle
a jumble, a muddle, especially of twisted threads or hair.

tank
1 a container to hold large amounts of liquid or gas.
2 a large vehicle which is used in war and is able to move over very rough country.

tanker
a ship or lorry which carries liquids such as petrol or oil.

tap
1 a knob or handle which is turned to allow liquids to flow.
2 a tiny knock.

tape
1 a narrow piece of material, such as cloth or sticky tape, often used to hold things together.
2 a long, narrow strip of plastic material used for recording sounds.

tape recorder
a machine for making a copy of sounds and playing them back.

tall

tangerine

tangle

tapestry

tapestry
    pictures or patterns in silk or cotton worked on heavy cloth.

tar
    a thick, black liquid used in making roads.

target
    something at which you aim.

tart
    a piece of pastry filled with jam or fruit, for example.

tartan
    woollen cloth with a pattern of stripes and squares, often used in Scotland for making kilts.

task
    a piece of work which has to be done, a job.

taste
    1 the flavour of food or drink.
    2 to try a little food or drink.

tasty
    nice to eat.

tax
    money which has to be paid to the government.

taxi
    a car that can be hired by paying the driver.

tea
    a hot drink made from the dried leaves of the tea plant.

teach
    to help to learn, to give lessons to.

teacher
    a person who teaches.

team
    1 a number of people who work or play together.
    2 a number of animals working together.

tear (say 'teer')
    a drop of water from the eyes.

tear (say 'tare')
    to pull apart, to rip.

target

taxi

tears

a b c d e f g h i j k l m n o p q r s t u v w x y z

tease

tease
> to make fun of.

teenager
> a person aged between thirteen and nineteen years old.

telephone
> a way of carrying the sound of someone's voice by wire, using electricity.

telescope
> an instrument which you look through to see things that are far away.

television
> an instrument that brings sound and pictures through the air from long distances.

tell
> to give information in words, to say.

temper
> 1 the state of the mind, the mood you are in.
> 2 when you are very angry or annoyed about something.

temperature
> the amount of warmth or cold.

tempt
> to persuade someone to try to do what they really do not wish to do.

tend
> 1 to look after.
> 2 to be likely to.

tender
> 1 gentle, kind, showing love.
> 2 not tough, soft.
> 3 feeling painful.

tennis
> a game played by two or four people who use rackets to hit a ball over a net.

tent
> a waterproof shelter held up by poles and ropes.

term
> a part of the school or college year.

telephone

temperature

tent

terrace

terrace
   1 a flat, raised piece of ground.
   2 a row of houses joined together.

terrible
   very bad.

terrier
   a kind of small dog.

terrific
   very good, excellent.

terrify
   to frighten badly, to fill with fear.

terror
   great fear, great fright.

test
   to try out (for example, by looking at carefully).

thank
   to say that you are pleased about something that someone has given to you or done for you.

thatch
   a roof covering made of straw or reeds.

thaw
   1 (of snow and ice) to melt.
   2 warmer weather which melts snow and ice.

theatre
   1 a building where plays are acted, for example.
   2 a room in a hospital where operations take place.

theft
   stealing, robbing.

thermometer
   an instrument that measures heat and cold.

thick
   1 not thin, wide, deep.
   2 with a lot of things close together.
   3 (of a liquid) not flowing easily.

thief
   a person who steals.

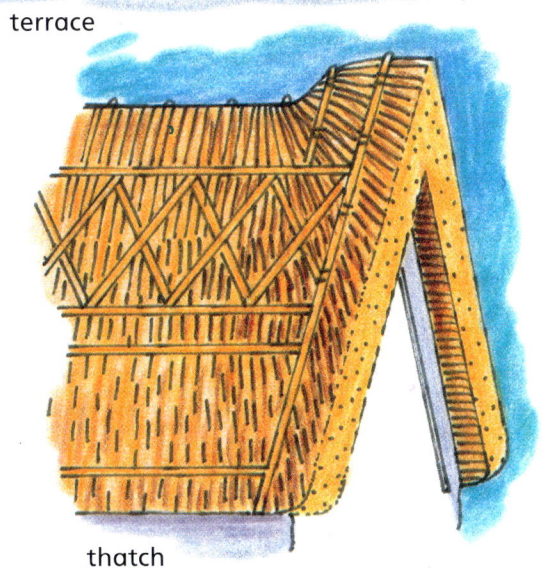

terrace

thatch

thaw

a b c d e f g h i j k l m n o p q r s t u v w x y z

thigh

thigh
   the part of the leg between the hip and the knee.

thimble
   a hard covering worn on the finger to protect it when you are sewing.

thin
   1 narrow, not fat.
   2 (of a liquid) flowing easily.

think
   to use the mind; to believe.

thirsty
   needing or wanting to drink.

thistle
   a kind of wild plant with prickly leaves and purple flowers.

thorn
   a prickle or point on a plant stem.

thorough
   1 taking great care that everything is done.
   2 complete.

thought
   thinking; an idea in the mind.

thread
   a very thin line of material used in sewing, knitting or weaving.

threat
   saying or showing that you mean to harm or punish someone.

thrilling
   very exciting.

throat
   the front part of the neck containing the tubes through which you swallow and breathe.

throb
   a strong, steady beat.

throne
   a special chair, usually for a king or queen.

through
   1 from one side to the other; from one end to the other.
   2 because of.

thorn

thread

thrilling

ABCDEFGHIJKLMNOPQRSTUVWXYZ

throw

throw
to make something from your hand move through the air.

thrush
a brown songbird with a spotted breast.

thrust
1 to push hard.
2 the lifting power of an engine (for example, of a rocket).

thud
the noise of something falling or bumping heavily.

thumb
the shortest and thickest finger of the hand.

thump
1 a heavy blow, usually struck with the fist.
2 a dull noise made by this.

thunder
the crash of noise that follows lightning.

tick
1 a mark ✓ to show, for example, that something has been checked or is correct.
2 the small, regular sound made by a clock or watch.

ticket
a card or paper allowing you to go into a place or to travel by train, aeroplane or bus.

tickle
to touch someone lightly to make them laugh.

tide
the rising and falling of the sea twice each day.

tidy
neat and in good order, properly arranged.

tie
1 a narrow piece of cloth worn round the neck.
2 to fasten (for example, by making a knot).
3 to be equal in a competition or test.

ticket

tidy

tie

a b c d e f g h i j k l m n o p q r s **t** u v w x y z

tiger

tiger
a large, Asian wild animal of the cat family with black-and-orange striped fur.

tight
fixed or fitting closely together.

tights
a piece of clothing which covers the feet, legs and lower part of the body.

tile
a flat piece of baked clay or plastic used, for example, to cover roofs, floors or walls.

till
1 until.
2 a drawer for holding money in a shop.

tilt
to lean to one side.

timber
wood for making things.

time
1 the passing of minutes, hours, days, months and years.
2 the hour of the day shown on the clock.

timid
easily frightened, likely to be afraid, shy.

tin
1 a silvery-white metal.
2 a metal can.

tingle
a prickly feeling often caused by cold, fear or excitement.

tinkle
a sound like that of a small bell.

tinsel
glittering material used for decoration.

tiny
very, very small.

tip
1 the pointed end of something.
2 to upset something.
3 to give money for something done.

tiptoe
to walk on the toes.

tight

till

tiny

222 **ABCDEFGHIJKLMNOPQRSTUVWXYZ**

tired

tired
  needing a rest.

tissue
  1 a piece of soft paper for wiping.
  2 very thin paper used for wrapping.

title
  1 the name of something (for example, a book or a piece of music).
  2 the first part of a name which shows the person's rank (for example, **Lord** Nelson).

toad
  an animal like a large frog with a rough skin.

toadstool
  a kind of plant shaped like an umbrella; many of them are poisonous.

toast
  bread which has been made crisp and brown by heat.

tobacco
  a plant from which the leaves are taken and used for smoking.

toboggan
  a light sledge for sliding on snow, especially down slopes, as a game.

today
  this day.

toddler
  a very young child who is just beginning to walk.

toe
  one of the five end parts of the foot.

toffee
  a sticky sweet made from sugar and butter.

together
  1 with someone or something.
  2 at the same time.

toilet
  1 a large bowl used for waste matter from the body.
  2 a room with a toilet.

tired

toast

toboggan

a b c d e f g h i j k l m n o p q r s **t** u v w x y z 223

tomato

tomato
a soft, round, red fruit, often eaten in salads.

tomb (rhymes with 'room')
a grave.

tomorrow
the day after today.

ton
a large measure of weight.

tone
1 the sound of the voice used in speaking or singing; the sound of a musical instrument.
2 a shade of colour.

tongue
the thick, soft part inside the mouth used for tasting, eating and speaking.

tonight
this night.

tonne
a large measure of mass, equal to 1000 kilograms.

tonsils
two small lumps at the back of the throat.

tool
an instrument used to help you to do some work.

tooth
one of the hard parts growing out of the jaw, used for biting and chewing.

toothache
a pain in a tooth.

top
1 the highest part, above all others.
2 a covering or lid for something (for example a bottle).
3 a toy which spins.

torch
1 an electric light which can be carried about.
2 a burning stick carried to give light.

torment
to cause pain to someone, to tease, to annoy.

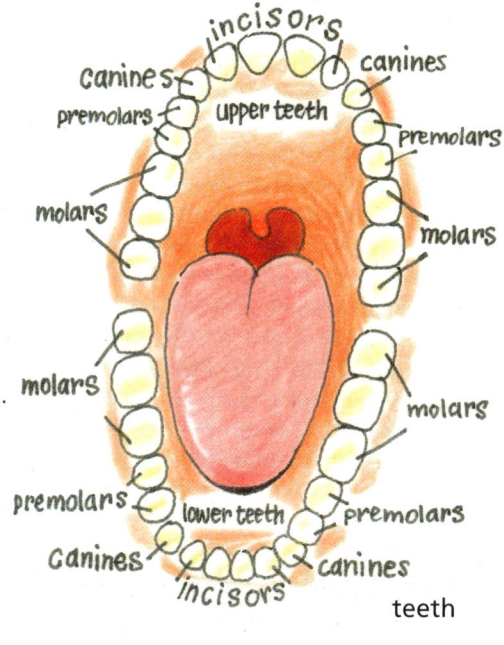

tools

teeth

torch

torment

torment
great pain and suffering.

torpedo
a weapon which can be fired through water, usually against ships.

tortoise
a kind of slow-moving animal with a hard, round shell.

torture
to cause great pain to someone on purpose.

toss
to throw into the air.

total
everything added together, the whole.

touch
1 to be as close as possible to something.
2 to feel gently with the hand or another part of the body.

tough
hard, strong; not easy to bite or cut.

tour
a journey in which you visit a number of places.

tourist
a person who travels for pleasure.

tow
to pull something along using a rope or chain (for example, a car or a boat).

towards
in the direction of.

towel
a piece of cloth for drying wet things.

tower
a tall, narrow building or part of a building.

town
a large number of houses and other buildings grouped together, smaller than a city but larger than a village.

toy
something you play with.

tortoise

toss

tourist

a b c d e f g h i j k l m n o p q r s **t** u v w x y z 225

trace

trace
1 a very small amount left behind.
2 to copy exactly by following the lines of a drawing, for example, through transparent paper.
3 to find after searching and following clues.

track
1 a narrow path.
2 a place specially prepared for races.
3 the metal lines on which a train runs.
4 a mark left by a foot or a tyre, for example.

track suit
loose trousers and a top sometimes worn over sports clothes.

tractor
a strong machine for pulling heavy loads, used especially on a farm.

trade
1 buying and selling.
2 a job, especially one in which you use your hands.

traffic
movement of vehicles and people.

tragedy
something very sad that happens.

trail
1 to follow the track or the scent of an animal.
2 to drag or be dragged behind.

trailer
1 a cart or box on wheels which is pulled by a vehicle.
2 a short piece of a film or video to make you interested in the full film or video.

train
1 railway coaches joined to an engine.
2 the back part of a dress which trails on the ground.
3 to guide or teach someone to do something.

tractor

traffic

train

A B C D E F G H I J K L M N O P Q R S T U V W X Y Z

trainer

trainer
a kind of shoe which may be worn for sports.

traitor
a person who secretly helps an enemy of his or her country, for example.

tramp
1 a person with no home or job who wanders from place to place.
2 to walk heavily.

trample
to walk heavily on, often doing damage.

trampoline
a large frame with springs covered with material on which you can bounce up and down.

transparent
able to be seen through.

transport
the moving of things or people from place to place.

trap
1 something which is made to catch an animal or bird, for example.
2 to catch in a clever way.

trapeze
a bar joining two ropes which hang down to make a swing in a circus or gym.

travel
to move from one place to another.

trawler
a fishing boat which catches fish by dragging a large net in the sea.

tray
a flat piece of wood, plastic or metal for carrying small things.

treacle
a dark, sweet, sticky liquid made from sugar.

treasure
something of great value.

trampoline

transparent

trawler

a b c d e f g h i j k l m n o p q r s **t** u v w x y z   227

treasurer

treasurer
a person who looks after the money which belongs to a group of people.

treat
1 to behave or act towards in a certain way.
2 something specially pleasant you are given.

tree
a large plant with a trunk, branches and leaves.

tremble
to shiver, to shake with excitement, fear or cold.

trespass
to go into a private place without permission.

trial
1 a test.
2 an examination before a judge to decide whether or not a person is guilty.

triangle
1 a flat shape with three straight sides and three corners, like this △.
2 a metal musical instrument of this shape, played by striking it with a steel rod.

tribe
a group of people ruled by one chief.

trick
1 to cheat.
2 something clever done either to cheat or to amuse people.

trickle
a very small flow of liquid.

tricycle
a cycle with three wheels.

trifle
1 a small thing of no importance.
2 a kind of pudding made of cake, custard, fruit and cream.

trigger
a small lever which is pulled to fire a gun.

trespass

trickle

trifle

trim

trim
1 tidy, neat.
2 to cut and make tidy.

trio
a group of three people doing something together (for example, singing or playing instruments).

trip
1 a journey, especially one for pleasure.
2 to stumble and fall.

triumph
a great victory or success.

trolley
1 a small, light cart pushed by hand.
2 a small table with wheels, used for serving food.

trombone
a long, brass musical instrument which you play by blowing.

troop
a large group of people or animals.

troops
soldiers.

trot
to run gently with short steps.

trouble
1 a worry, a problem, a difficulty.
2 to cause worry or annoyance to.

trousers
a piece of clothing for the legs and lower part of the body.

trout
a kind of fish that lives in fresh water.

trowel
1 a garden tool like a small spade.
2 a small, flat-bladed tool for spreading cement, for example.

truant
a person who stays away from school without permission.

truck
a vehicle for carrying heavy loads.

trip

trolley

trombone

a b c d e f g h i j k l m n o p q r s t u v w x y z   229

trudge

trudge
: to walk slowly and heavily as you do when you are tired.

true
: correct, honest.

trumpet
: a brass musical instrument which you play by blowing.

trunk
: 1 the thick stem of a tree.
  2 a large box for carrying things, especially on a journey.
  3 an elephant's long nose.
  4 the body (without the head, arms and legs).

trunks
: shorts or pants worn by men and boys for swimming.

trust
: 1 to believe that someone is honest and can be relied on.
  2 to believe to be true.

truth
: what is true.

try
: 1 to make an effort to do something.
  2 to test.

T-shirt
: a light, cotton shirt with short sleeves.

tub
: a round container with an open top.

tube
: 1 a thin pipe.
  2 a soft metal or plastic container from which the contents can be squeezed.
  3 an underground railway, especially in London.

tuck
: to push or put something into or under something.

tuft
: a small bunch of grass, hair or feathers, for example.

trunk

the tube

tuft

230 A B C D E F G H I J K L M N O P Q R S **T** U V W X Y Z

tug

tug
1 to pull hard and sharply.
2 a small, powerful boat used to pull other boats.

tulip
a kind of bell-shaped spring flower grown from a bulb.

tumble
to fall heavily.

tumbler
a flat-bottomed drinking glass.

tuna
a kind of very large fish found in warm seas.

tune
a set of pleasant musical notes.

tunnel
a long, covered passageway through hills or under rivers.

turban
a covering for the head made from a long strip of material wound in a special way.

turf
short grass with its roots and the earth in which it grows.

turkey
a kind of large bird kept on farms.

turn
1 to face a different way; to move round.
2 to change direction.
3 a chance to do something after other people (for example, in a game).

turnip
a kind of root vegetable with white or yellowish flesh.

turquoise
1 a greenish-blue precious stone.
2 the colour of this stone.

turret
a small tower in a building.

turtle
an animal which has a hard, round shell and lives mainly in the sea.

tug

turban

turkey

a b c d e f g h i j k l m n o p q r s t u v w x y z 231

tusk

tusk
    a long, pointed tooth found in some animals such as an elephant or a walrus.

tweed
    a kind of rough woollen cloth (used for suits and heavy coats, for example).

tweezers
    a small tool used to get hold of things.

twice
    two times.

twig
    a very small branch of a tree.

twin
    one of two babies born at the same time to the same mother.

twinkle
    to shine with small, bright flashes.

twirl
    to twist round, to spin quickly.

twist
    1 to wind things round each other.
    2 to turn (a bottle cap, for example).

twitch
    to move suddenly and quickly.

twitter
    chirping sounds, like those made by birds.

type
    1 a special sort, a kind.
    2 to tap keys on a typewriter or keyboard in order to print words.

typewriter
    a machine with keys used to print words on paper.

typhoon
    a great storm.

tyre
    the rubber round the outside of a wheel, usually filled with air.

tweezers

type

typhoon

U u

ugly
not nice to look at.

umbrella
a covering you hold over your head to keep off the rain.

umpire
the person who makes sure that a game is played fairly, a referee.

uncle
the brother of a father or mother; an aunt's husband.

under
below.

underground
1 under the earth.
2 a railway which goes under the ground.

understand
to know what something means.

underwear
clothes worn next to the skin under other clothes.

undo
to untie.

unemployed
having no paid work.

unfair
not fair.

unfold
to open out something folded.

unhappy
not happy.

unicorn
an imaginary animal like a horse, with one horn.

umbrella

umpire

undo

uniform

uniform
special clothing worn by people of the same group, such as the police, soldiers or nurses.

unique
the only one of its kind.

unit
1 one complete thing or set.
2 an amount used as a measurement.

unite
to join together into one.

universe
all the suns and planets in space.

university
a place where people may go to learn after leaving school.

unload
to take something off (a lorry, for example).

unlock
to open with a key.

unpack
to take things out of a case or container.

untie
to loosen a knot (in string, for example).

until
up to the time of, till.

unwell
ill.

up
to a higher place.

upon
on, on top of.

upright
1 standing straight up.
2 honest and trustworthy.

uproar
a lot of loud noise and excitement.

upset
1 to make others unhappy.
2 to turn over, to knock down.

unique

unload

unwell

upside down

upside down
   the wrong way up.
upstairs
   on a higher floor of a building.
upwards
   up to a higher place.
urgent
   of great importance so that it needs to be done at once.
use (say 'yooz')
   to do something with.
use (say 'yoos')
   what you do with something.
useful
   of some use, helpful.
useless
   of no use, not useful.
usual
   often done; happening often.

upside down

useless

upwards

a b c d e f g h i j k l m n o p q r s t **u** v w x y z   235

V v

vacant
 empty.
vacuum
 1 a space with no air in it.
 2 **vacuum cleaner** a machine for lifting dirt out of carpets, for example.
 3 **vacuum flask** a container for keeping liquids hot or cold.
vague
 not certain or clear.
vain
 1 too proud, conceited.
 2 **in vain** uselessly.
valley
 low ground between two hills or mountains.
valuable
 worth a lot.
value
 the importance you put on something, its price.
van
 1 a covered vehicle for carrying goods.
 2 a railway coach for luggage and parcels.
vanilla
 a sweet flavouring used in ice cream, for example.
vanish
 to go out of sight, to disappear.
variety
 1 many different things mixed together.
 2 a kind.
various
 different.
varnish
 a transparent substance painted on a surface to protect it.

vacuum cleaner

valley

valuable

vary

vary
   to be or make different, to change.
vase
   a container for holding flowers.
vast
   very large, of great size.
vault
   to jump over something.
vegetable
   a plant grown for food (for example, carrots or cabbage).
vegetarian
   a person who chooses not to eat meat or fish.
vehicle
   something such as a cart, car or van used for carrying people or things.
veil
   a thin covering for the face or head, usually to hide it.
vein
   one of the thin tubes which carry blood round the body to the heart.
velvet
   a kind of cloth which is soft and smooth on one side.
verdict
   what is decided, especially in a law court.
verge
   the edge of a road or path.
verse
   1 poetry.
   2 part of a poem.
   3 a small section from the Bible.
vertical
   straight up, standing upright, at right angles to the horizon.
vessel
   1 a container for liquids.
   2 a ship.
vest
   a piece of clothing worn next to the skin on the top part of the body.

vase

vault

veil

vet

vet
    an animal doctor.

vicar
    (in the Church of England) a priest who is in charge of a church.

vicious
    very bad, very wicked.

victim
    a person who has suffered because of what other people have done to him or her or because of illness or an accident.

victory
    when a person or a group of people beats others in battle or in a competition.

video
    1 a film for showing on a television set.
    2 a machine which records and plays back films and television programmes.

view
    1 what you can see.
    2 what you think about something.

village
    a number of houses grouped together, a small town.

villain
    a wicked person, a rascal.

vinegar
    a sour liquid used for flavouring and for preserving food.

violence
    1 great force.
    2 wild, hurtful behaviour.

violet
    1 a kind of tiny bluish-purple flower.
    2 a bluish-purple colour, one of the colours of the rainbow.

violin
    a stringed musical instrument held under the chin and played with a bow.

virus
    a very small living thing in the blood that often causes illness.

visible
    able to be seen.

vicar

village

violin

vision

vision
 1 sight.
 2 something seen in a dream.

visit
 to call to see someone or something.

vital
 necessary for life, very important.

vivid
 bright and clear.

vocabulary
 the words used in speaking and writing.

voice
 the sound made by the mouth when speaking or singing.

volcano
 a mountain which sometimes throws out melting rock, hot ashes, steam and flames.

volleyball
 a game in which a ball is played back and forward over a net by hand.

volume
 1 the space something fills.
 2 a book.
 3 how loud a sound is.

voluntary
 done freely and openly.

volunteer
 a person who offers to do something.

vomit
 to be sick.

vote
 to make a choice, to choose at an election.

vow
 a solemn promise.

voyage
 a long journey, usually by sea.

vulgar
 rude, not polite.

vulture
 a kind of large, powerful bird which feeds on dead animals.

volcano

volleyball

vote

a b c d e f g h i j k l m n o p q r s t u **v** w x y z

W w

waddle
 to walk like a duck.

wade
 to walk through water.

wafer
 a very thin biscuit, often eaten with ice cream.

wag
 to move something from side to side.

wage
 money given for work done, often paid weekly.

wagon, waggon
 1 a vehicle for carrying heavy loads.
 2 a railway truck.

wail
 to make a long, high-pitched cry.

waist
 the middle of the body, just above the hips.

wait
 to stay in a place for a reason.

waiter
 a man who serves food in a restaurant or café.

waitress
 a woman who serves food in a restaurant or café.

wake
 1 to stop sleeping.
 2 the foam made in the sea behind a ship.

walk
 to move on the feet.

wall
 bricks or stones making a fence or part of a building.

wag

wait

wake

ABCDEFGHIJKLMNOPQRSTUVWXYZ

wallet

wallet
a small, flat case for holding paper money, usually carried in the pocket.

walnut
1 a kind of nut.
2 the tree it grows on; the wood is used for making furniture.

walrus
a water animal like a large seal with two long tusks.

waltz
a graceful dance for two people.

wand
a thin, straight stick used by magicians.

wander
to roam about.

want
to wish to have.

war
fighting between countries or large groups of people.

ward
a room at a hospital with beds.

warden
a person who looks after a place (for example, a building or a nature reserve).

warder
a person who looks after prisoners in a jail.

wardrobe
a cupboard for storing clothes.

warm
fairly hot.

warn
to tell someone of difficulty or danger which may appear.

warrior
a fighter, a soldier.

wart
a small, hard lump on the skin.

wash
to clean using water.

wallet

walrus

wash

wasp

wasp
  a black-and-yellow striped insect with a painful sting.

waste
  1 useless things.
  2 to spoil or use carelessly.

watch
  1 a small clock, usually worn on the wrist.
  2 to look at carefully.
  3 to guard.

watchman
  a man who looks after a place.

water
  the liquid that is found in rivers and in the sea and falls as rain.

waterfall
  a stream or river falling from a height.

waterproof
  made of material through which water cannot go.

wave
  1 a higher part of the moving surface of water.
  2 to move the hand and arm from side to side.
  3 a curl in your hair.

wax
  something which melts easily, used to make candles, for example.

way
  1 how you do something.
  2 a road or path.

weak
  not strong.

wealthy
  having a lot of money.

weapon
  a tool you use to fight or hunt with.

wear
  1 to have on (clothes, for example).
  2 to become damaged by a lot of use.

weary
  very tired.

watchman

waterfall

waterproof

weasel

weasel
a kind of small, furry wild animal with a long body.

weather
how sunny, cold or wet, for example, it is outside.

weave
to make cloth by twisting threads over and under each other.

web
the thin net made by a spider to catch flies.

wedding
when two people get married.

wedge
a piece of wood, for example, which is thinner at one end than the other.

weed
1 a wild plant which grows where it is not wanted.
2 to dig out weeds.

week
seven days.

weep
to have tears in your eyes, to cry.

weigh
1 to measure how heavy something is.
2 to be a certain weight.

weight
how heavy something is, mass.

weird
very strange.

welcome
to show you are happy because someone has come.

well
1 a deep hole holding water.
2 in good health.
3 in a good way.

wellingtons
long, rubber boots.

west
the direction where the sun sets.

weather

weigh

well

a b c d e f g h i j k l m n o p q r s t u v **w** x y z   243

wet

wet
   having a lot of liquid in it or on it.

whale
   the largest kind of sea animal.

wheat
   a plant producing grain which is used to make flour.

wheel
   1 a ring of metal, plastic or wood which turns and helps things move more easily.
   2 to push something that has wheels.

whimper
   to cry softly.

whine
   1 a long, sad cry like the cry of a dog.
   2 to complain a lot without good reason.

whip
   1 a piece of thin leather or cord on a handle, used for hitting things.
   2 to beat.

whirl
   to spin round quickly.

whiskers
   hair on the face (for example, the long, stiff hair at the side of a cat's mouth).

whisper
   to speak very quietly.

whistle
   1 a high, shrill note made by blowing through the lips and teeth.
   2 an instrument for making a high note.

white
   1 the colour of clean snow.
   2 the part of an egg round the yolk.

whole
   complete, with nothing missing.

wick
   the string which burns in candles and oil lamps.

wicked
   very bad, evil.

wicket
   the three stumps at cricket.

wheat

whiskers

whistle

ABCDEFGHIJKLMNOPQRSTUVWXYZ

wide

wide
    not narrow, broad.

widow
    a woman whose husband is dead.

widower
    a man whose wife is dead.

wife
    a married woman.

wig
    false hair to cover the head.

wigwam
    a North American Indian tent or hut.

wild
    1 not tame, fierce.
    2 not looked after by people.
    3 out of control.

wilderness
    a large, wild area where no one lives.

will
    1 a written piece of paper saying who is to have a person's belongings when they are dead.
    2 the power to choose what you want to do.

willow
    a kind of tree with thin, drooping branches.

win
    to be first or to do best in a competition, race or fight.

wind (rhymes with 'pinned')
    air which is moving quickly.

wind (rhymes with 'mind')
    to turn round and round.

windmill
    a building with a machine which is turned by the wind.

window
    an opening in the wall of a building to let light in.

wigwam

willow

windmill

wine

wine
    a strong drink made from the juice of crushed fruit, usually grapes.

wing
    1 one of the parts which are used for flying by a bird or an insect.
    2 one of the two parts of an aeroplane which keep it in the air.

wink
    to shut and open one eye.

winter
    the coldest season of the year, between autumn and spring.

wipe
    to dry or clean with a cloth.

wire
    thin, metal thread.

wisdom
    being wise.

wise
    showing good sense, clever, understanding a lot.

wish
    1 to want something very much and to hope to get it.
    2 what you wish for.

wit
    cleverness, quickness of mind.

witch
    a woman who is supposed to have magic powers.

wither
    to become smaller, drier and paler.

witness
    1 a person who sees something happen.
    2 to see something happen.

wizard
    a man who is supposed to have magic powers.

wobble
    to move unsteadily from one side to the other.

wine

wink

wither

A B C D E F G H I J K L M N O P Q R S T U V W X Y Z

wolf

wolf
   a wild animal like a large dog.

woman
   an adult female person.

wonder
   1 to be surprised at.
   2 to want to know.

wonderful
   very good or pleasant, amazing.

wood
   1 a lot of trees growing together.
   2 the material which trees are made of.

wool
   1 the short, curly hair on the backs of sheep and lambs.
   2 thread made from this, used in weaving or knitting.

woollen
   made of wool.

word
   letters together which mean something when spoken or read.

work
   something you do, especially for payment, a job.

world
   the earth; all human beings together.

worm
   a long, thin animal which has a soft body and lives in soil.

worn
   when something has been used so much that it is of little further use.

worry
   to feel anxious about something.

worse
   not as good as, less well.

worth
   value.

wound
   an injury where the skin is cut.

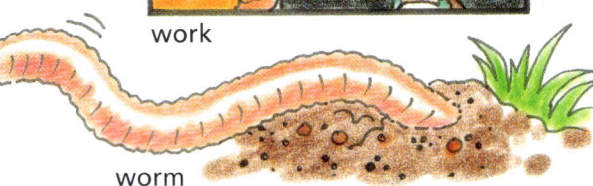

wood

work

worm

a b c d e f g h i j k l m n o p q r s t u v **w** x y z

wrap

wrap
to put a covering closely round something.
wreck
to smash up completely.
wren
a kind of very small, brown bird.
wrestle
to struggle with a person and try to throw him or her to the ground, sometimes as a sport.
wriggle
to twist the body about.
wring
to twist and squeeze something tightly to get water out.
wrinkle
a line or crease on the skin or in material.
wrist
the joint between the hand and the arm.
write
to put words or letters on paper so that they can be read and understood.
wrong
not right, not correct.

wrap

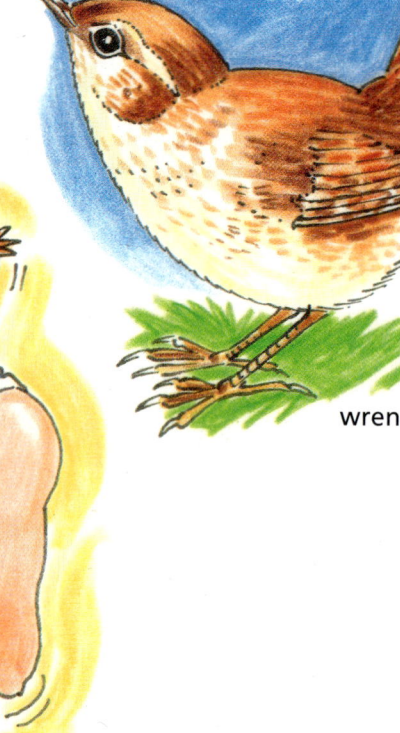

wren

wring

ABCDEFGHIJKLMNOPQRSTUVWXYZ

Xx

X-ray
a special photograph of the inside of your body, for example.

xylophone
a musical instrument played by hitting bars of wood or metal with a small hammer.

X-ray

xylophone

Yy

yacht
   a light sailing boat, often used for racing.

yard
   1 a measure of length.
   2 a piece of ground which is next to a building and has a fence or wall around it.

yawn
   to open the mouth and breathe in and out deeply, when tired or bored.

year
   a period of time equal to twelve months; the time that the earth takes to go once round the sun.

yeast
   something used in baking bread to make the dough rise, and also in making beer or wine

yell
   to shout very loudly.

yellow
   the colour of a lemon or the yolk of an egg.

yesterday
   the day before today.

yew
   a kind of evergreen tree with red berries.

yoghurt, yogurt
   a sour food made from milk, sometimes flavoured with fruit and sugar.

yoke
   a piece of wood put across the necks of cattle (for pulling carts, for example).

yolk
   the yellow centre part of an egg.

young
   not old.

yacht

yawn

yoke

ABCDEFGHIJKLMNOPQRSTUVWXYZ

youth

youth
 1 the time when you are young.
 2 a young man.

yo-yo
 a toy which moves up and down on a string.

yo-yo

youth

a b c d e f g h i j k l m n o p q r s t u v w x **y z**

Zz

zebra
 an African animal like a small horse with black and white stripes.

zebra crossing
 a specially-marked part of the street for people crossing.

zero
 the number 0, nothing.

zigzag
 to move sharply to one side and then to the other.

zip
 a sliding fastener used on clothes.

zoo
 a place where wild animals are kept so that people can look at them.

zebra

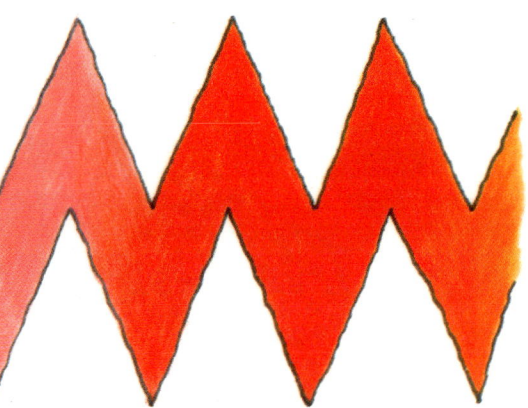

zigzag

zip

ABCDEFGHIJKLMNOPQRSTUVWXYZ